Nelson Gómez E.

THE POCKET GUIDE TO ECUADOR

Printed by **EDIGUIAS C. Ltda.**
Galo Plaza Lasso Av. (10 de Agosto Av.) N54-150 and Los Pinos
Faxphone: (593 2) 40 40 37 / E-Mail: ciesa@pi.pro.ec
P.O.Box 17-08-8310 / Quito - Ecuador

ISBN 9978-89-018-1

1998 Edition

OTHER GUIDES BY NELSON GÓMEZ:

Ecuador Road Atlas
(Guía Vial del Ecuador)

Quito Street Guide
(Guía Informativa de Quito)

Quito Pocket Guide
(Quito, Guía de bolsillo)

Quito Tourist Plan
(in English and Spanish)

Guayaquil Street Guide
(Guía Informativa de Guayaquil)

Guayaquil Pocket Guide
(Guayaquil, Guía de bolsillo)

Cuenca Pocket Guide
(Cuenca, Guía de bolsillo)

Galapagos Pocket Guide
(in English)

Otavalo Pocket Guide
(in English)

Province of Pichincha's Guide
(Guía de la Provincia de Pichincha)

Original text, maps and coordination:
Nelson Gómez E.
Graphic design:
Beatrice Gómez L.
Layout and maps:
Mercy González and Patricio Cajo
Photo offset:
José Bucheli
Printing:
John Barrera and Abel Guacho
English text:
Robert and Daisy Kunstaetter
Susana Echeverría T.

All of the maps and plans have been taken from the guides Vial, Quito, Guayaquil, and Cuenca which have the I.G.M. (Instituto Geográfico Militar) authorization.

TABLE OF CONTENTS

INTRODUCTION

ORIGINS

Only four decades after Christopher Columbus' arrival in the new world in 1492, a group of Spanish explorers headed by Francisco Pizarro discovered the tropical Pacific coastline of South America. This territory was at the time part of the vast Inca empire, stretching from what is today the south of Colombia to northern Chile, a length of some 3.300 km. (2.050 miles). From the Pacific shoreline to the summits of the Andes and their eastern slopes descending to the Amazon Jungle, the *Tahuantinsuyo*, as this empire was called, varied in width from 200 to 300 km. (125 to 190 mi.). The inhabitants of this region were a heterogeneous group of peoples, composed of many different cultures and tribes which had been conquered by the Incas and amalgamated into their great empire.

By the time of the Spanish conquest, the *Tahuantinsuyo* had grown so large that it was divided into two halves. The northern half, including what is today Ecuador, was ruled by *Atahualpa* from the city of Quito. The southern half was ruled by his brother *Huáscar* from Cuzco in present-day Peru. Dividing the empire among his two sons proved to be the great error of their father, the emperor *Huayna-Cápac*. The brothers soon quarreled setting off a bloody civil war which weakened the once mighty empire, facilitating its conquest by the newly arrived Europeans and its subjugation to the Spanish Crown.

In 1563 the *Real Audiencia* (Crown Colony) of Quito was established with the city of the same name as its capital. There followed three centuries of less than benign Spanish colonial rule. On August 10, 1809, patriots in Quito gave the first cry of independence in Latin America which ushered in several years of war against Spain. These culminated on May 24, 1822, with the battle of Pichincha in which General Antonio José de Sucre won a decisive victory in favor of the forces of independence.

The newly independent country took its name from the equator which crosses its territory and which was a subject of much interest in European scientific circles of the time. As early as 1736 a scientific mission had been dispatched to Quito by the Academy of Sciences in Paris in order to carry out astronomical measurements aimed at establishing the true shape of the planet. As the eagerly awaited data began to arrive in Europe, it brought with it ever increasing awareness of the lands in equatorial South America. So it was that in order to seek international recognition, the Constitutional Assembly of 1830 unanimously adopted the name of Ecuador for the new republic.

GEOGRAPHY

Ecuador is located in the north-west of South America, lying along the Pacific coast and, naturally, the equator. The principal topographic feature of the country is the massive mountain range which runs from north to south, dividing the. Ecuadorian mainland into three principal geographic regions: the Pacific coast, the Andes mountains, and the Amazon jungle. A fourth geographic region is made up of the Galápagos Islands situated about 1.000 km. (620 miles) offshore, directly along the equator.

THE PACIFIC COASTAL REGION

Is a broad alluvial plain drained by the largest river on South America's west coast, the Guayas. This alluvial plain measures 550 km. (340 mi.) in length and varies between 50 and 200 km. (30 and 120 mi.) in width. It is crossed by a chain of low mountains rising 800 m. (2.800 ft.) above sea level, running parallel to the coast between the provinces of Esmeraldas in the north and Guayas in the south. The Gulf of Guayaquil forms a wedge with its apex driven into the coastal plain.

Due to the combined influences of warm and cold Pacific Ocean currents, the climate in coastal Ecuador is most varied, with very high precipitation (5000 mm. or 195 in. annual rainfall) in the north and semi-desert conditions (300 mm. or 12 in.) in the south. Along the beaches of the Santa Elena peninsula, the months of July and August are cool, whereas inland temperatures on the coastal plain remain high year-round and may reach extreme levels from January through May.

Much of the coastal plain is given over to agriculture, with large corporate enterprises producing bananas and shrimp for the export market. Other crops include cocoa, rice, coffee, sugar cane, beef cattle and a large variety of tropical fruits.

THE ANDEAN REGION

May also be classified into northern and southern sections. The north is a land of snow-capped active volcanoes towering to over 6.000 m. (20.000 ft.) above sea level. In the south the mountains are older and more eroded, resulting in a confused topography of hills and valleys.

Ecuador in general, and the andean region in particular, is geothermally active giving rise to occasional volcanic eruptions, earth tremors, hot mineral springs, and related phenomena. The Ecuadorian Andes are a world of striking contrasts: massive glaciers on the equator, snow and volcanic steam, delicate alpine tundra and lush tropical forests, dense fog and brilliant sunshine, severe cold and intense heat. Perhaps they are a microcosm of the elemental forces of nature which have shaped our entire planet.

Between the two main ranges of the Andes, known as the central and western *cordilleras*, lie a series of broad valleys at about 2.500 m. (8.200 ft.) above sea level. These inter-andean valleys are intensively cultivated, producing fruits, vegetables, grains and dairy products. Their agricultural resources are managed with great skill by the indigenous population. The large *haciendas* (plantations) of the past have been transformed into smaller properties dedicated both to subsistence farming and to the production of export crops such as flowers. With only slight variations refered to as the wet (October to May) and dry (July to September) seasons, the climate of these valleys comes close to eternal spring. Sunrise and sunset in the Andes can be an unforgettable experience.

The shape of the gentle green inter-andean slopes is often a reminder of their harsh volcanic and heavily glaciated past. The craters of extinct volcanoes, worn down by thousands of years of glacial activity, have become giant cauldron-shaped valleys inhabited today by the highland Indians and their flocks. In addition to the remnants of ancient glacial moraines, there is evidence of more recent erosion as the rivers of the region, have carved great canyons along their courses. Yet another landscape is to be found on the external slopes of the Andes which are covered with unique cloud forests, known as *Ceja Andina* (the eyebrows of the Andes). They are perpetually shrouded in the mists which rise from the tropical lowlands towards the icy mountaintops.

THE ECUADORIAN AMAZON

Is part of the enormous river basin which covers much of tropical South America. Like the rest of the Amazon Jungle it has an extremely hot and humid climate and a unique flora and fauna which make it the most important rainforest on earth. Large navigable rivers are the principal means of transportation in this region which remains, for the moment, the least densely populated and most pristine of continental Ecuador's three geographic zones. However, petroleum exploration in the north of this area has been an important impetus for road construction and development, as well as having a significant impact on the environment, in Ecuador's Amazonía.

MOUNTAINS

The following is a list of Ecuador's major summits (from north to south) and their elevations:

	Meters	Feet
Chiles	4.720	15.482
Yanaurco de Piñán	4.535	14.875
Cotacachi	4.939	16.200
Imbabura	4.630	15.186
Cayambe	5.790	18.991

Reventador*	3.485	11.431
Saraurcu	4.676	15.337
Puntas	4.676	15.337
Rucu Pichincha	4.675	15.334
Guagua Pichincha*	4.794	15.724
Atacazo	4.457	14.619
Corazón	4.786	15.698
Antisana	5.705	18.712
Pasochoa	4.200	13.776
Sincholagua	4.898	16.065
Sumaco	3.900	12.792
Rumiñahui	4.712	15.455
Cotopaxi*	5.897	19.342
Quilindaña	4.878	16.000
Iliniza	5.266	17.272
Yanaurcu	4.292	14.078
Quilotoa*	4.000	13.120
Carihuairazo	5.020	16.466
Chimborazo	6.310	20.697
Tungurahua	5.016	16.452
Altar	5.319	17.446
Sangay*	5.230	17.154

***Active volcanoes**

POPULATION

By 1990 the population of Ecuador had reached 10 million inhabitants. The average birth-rate remains high, resulting in a great majority of young people in the demographic make-up of the country. Fifty-five per cent of the population is urban, forty-five percent is rural. The vast majority of people are concentrated along the coastal plain and in the inter-andean valleys, and both of these regions have a very high population density. The high mountains and the Amazon basin, on the other hand, remain sparsely populated.

CITIES

The nature of Ecuadorian cities and towns has, to a large extent, been determined by the geographic and climatic regions in which they are respectively located. Along the coast, the somewhat flimsy, erratic, construction typical of many tropical zones predominates. In the inter-andean region, houses tend to be more solid, and the cities (which are often older) have a more rigid, formal, structure. In the larger highland cities, strict construction standards require that all modern buildings be earthquake-proof. Many of the towns in the Amazon basin are only now growing large enough to develop a character of their own.

Ecuador's two most important cities are Quito, the capital, and Guayaquil, the largest metropolis and main port. Cuenca is third in population and a very important regional center in the southern highlands Andes.

These three are followed in importance by the provincial capitals and certain local centers, situated principally along the coastal plain.

The following is a list of Ecuador's cities and the population of their urban areas according to the 1990 census:

	Inhabitants
Guayaquil	1'508.444
Quito	1'100.847
Cuenca	194.981
Machala	144.197
Portoviejo	132.937
Manta	125.505
Ambato	124.166
Santo Domingo	114.422
Esmeraldas	98.558
Riobamba	95.505
Loja	94.305
Milagro	93.637
Quevedo	86.910
Durán	82.359
Ibarra	80.991
La Libertad	53.108
Babahoyo	50.285
Chone	41.437
Latacunga	39.882
Tulcán	37.069
Sangolquí	35.386
Calderón	34.514
Pasaje	32.947
Santa Rosa	32.648
Jipijapa	32.225
Huaquillas	27.368
Daule	24.399
El Empalme	24.112
Ventanas	23.217
El Carmen	22.870
Balzar	21.721
Otavalo	21.548
Azogues	21.060
La Troncal	19.654
Conocoto	19.450
Salinas	19.298
Vinces	17.512
Santa Elena	17.459
Cayambe	16.849
Playas	16.590
Buena Fe	16.508
El Triunfo	16.399
Rosa Zarate	16.171
Naranjito	16.131
Guaranda	15.730
Bahía de Caráquez	15.308
Naranjal	14.064

TRANSPORT & COMMUNICATIONS

Ecuador has two international airports located in Quito and Guayaquil respectively. Other airports offering national and regional service include those of Cuenca, Tulcán, Loja, San Lorenzo, Esmeraldas, Manta, Salinas, Machala, Shell (Puyo), Nueva Loja (Lago Agrio), Puerto Francisco Orellana (Coca), Puerto Baquerizo Moreno (San Cristóbal Island, Galápagos) and Baltra (access for Santa Cruz Island, Galápagos).

There is an extensive road network which links virtually the entire country, including many excellent paved highways. Most secondary roads are gravel and quite suitable for general use by ordinary vehicles. Some of the roads in more remote areas are graded earth and may require four-wheel-drive vehicles, especially in the rainy season. Prudence is advised for those unfamiliar with mountain driving and, just as anywhere else, excessive speed is best avoided. There are a number of international and local car rental agencies with offices in the main cities, renting sedan cars as well as four-wheel-drives. Frequently scheduled bus service is available throughout Ecuador.

International shipping service is provided through the following major Pacific ports: Guayaquil, Manta, Esmeraldas, and Puerto Bolívar (Machala). Local coastal and river transport is frequent and easily obtainable.

Railroad facilities are rudimentary but most picturesque and of considerable interest to many visitors. The world famous switchbacked railway pass through the Andes, known as *La Naríz del Diablo* (The Devil's Nose) has unfortunately been closed since 1983. Part of this journey can still be made however, on special equipment provided by a private tour company. Another spectacular rail trip is from Ibarra, in the highlands, down to San Lorenzo on the northern Pacific coast (see section on the province of Esmeraldas).

Postal service is available throughout the country although it may, on occasion, be a bit slow. Unfortunately, theft is all too common in the post office and goods or documents of value are best sent by private courier. National and international telephone service, telegrams, Telex, and Fax are widely available.

There are 4 major newspapers in Quito, 4 in Guayaquil, several regional papers and various nationwide television networks as well as countless radio stations throughout the country. Various international and foreign television networks are accessible through cable subscriber service in the major cities.

THE GOVERNMENT

For administrative purposes, Ecuador is divided into 21 provinces, which are subdivided into cantons and these in turn into parishes. Ecuador is a constitutional democracy and the current constitution dates to 1998. Voting is compulsory for all literate citizens ages 18 and over. The Ecuadorian government has three branches: executive, legislative and judicial. The executive is headed by the President and the Vice-President who are elected by direct ballot for a 4 year term. The judiciary branch is headed by the President of the Supreme Court of Justice who is appointed by Congress.

THE ECONOMY

Ecuador's traditional economic base has been the export of tropical fruits, particularly bananas. Other exports have included flowers, coffee, cocoa, rice, and sugar. More recently, shrimp farming has gained importance and Ecuador is today one of the largest exporters of shrimp in the world. Petroleum exports have also been very important in recent years and presently finance some 30% of the country's total expenditures.
Despite its small size, Ecuador is self-sufficient in virtually all of its population's basic needs. It has, to date, been spared the worst extremes of wealth and poverty found among some of its South American neighbors. None-theless, the country's resources are far from equitably distributed. An average Ecuadorian laborer earns the equivalent of US $70 a month.

Tourism continues to grow as increasing numbers of visitors are attracted by the country's natural beauty as well as by the warmth and sincerity of its inhabitants. The colonial city of Quito and the Galápagos Islands, both of which have been included in UNESCO's World Heritage Trust, remain the principal attractions. However both the region of the volcanoes and the Amazon Jungle, where several new national parks have been created, are continuing to grow in importance.

Handicrafts deserve a special mention as they hold a prominent place in the informal sector of the country's economy. Lovely textiles are produced throughout Ecuador in addition to crafts in wood, leather, clay, sea shells, and even bread-dough. It is not unusual for a region or town to specialize in one particular type of craft. Cuenca is particularly well known for its gold and silversmiths as well as ceramics and textiles.

Certain cities, such as Ambato, are important national commercial centers for a wide variety of agricultural products and manufactured goods. Other towns, such as Otavalo and Saquisilí, are known for their Indian markets and fairs. Throughout the country there are many bustling colorful marketplaces which are sure to catch the eye of the visitor.

CURRENCY

Ecuador's unit of currency is the *Sucre*, divided into 100 *centavos*. Both coins and bills, some of overlapping denominations, circulate. Counterfeiting has recently become something of a problem with the largest bills. Foreign exchange is available at most major hotels (poorest rates), many banks and *Casas de Cambio* (exchange houses). There are no restrictions on foreign exchange for tourists, nor is there a black market for foreign currency. Tourists are discouraged from dealing with street changers whose rates are generally no better than those of the *Casas de Cambio*.

PEOPLE

It is not surprising that the lifestyle of Ecuador's people varies with the geographic and climatic regions in which they live. The people of the highlands are generally more formal and traditional, often preserving the indigenous dress and customs of their ancestors. In the cool andean nights, the streets of towns and villages may be virtually deserted as folks retire early to the warmth of their homes. In the tropical lowlands, both along the Pacific coast and in the Amazon jungle, attire and behavior tend to be much less formal. Here, commercial activity may stop for several hours during the heat of midday and then continue amid a lively bustle late into the night. Compared to the reserved politeness of the highlanders, the lowland dwellers seem more open and vivacious.

There are two main cultural groups in Ecuador: the native indian people and the *mestizos*, people of mixed stock. There is also a small black community living principally in the Pacific coastal province of Esmeraldas, and small groups of european, middle-eastern, and oriental immigrants.
The highland indians are descendants of several ancient groups which were amalgamated into the *Quichua* culture with the Inca conquest of the region. The natives of the Andes maintain their traditional dress and a number of their ancestral customs. An important garment worn by the men is the *poncho*, a very warm woolen cape. The women wear an *anaco*, a long woolen skirt, colorfully embroidered blouses and a number of varieties of necklaces and bracelets.

Although the traditional adobe huts with straw roofs are gradually being replaced by homes made of bricks or cement blocks, these continue to have a single room, which is subdivided according to need. Meals are simple and they are based on traditional andean agricultural products such as potatoes, corn, millet *(quinua)* and lupins *(chochos)*. Alcoholic beverages are prepared by fermenting corn. These are drunk at all celebrations. Andean music is played on flutes and pan pipes *(rondadores)*, made of a bamboo like plant, known as *carrizo*.

Religious celebrations reflect a mixture of Catholicism and earlier pagan beliefs, in which the *Pacha Mama* (Mother Earth) holds a special importance. Many native people work in agriculture, on small subsistence farms or cooperatives. Others produce beautiful hand woven or knitted textiles for local consumption or for export and the tourist trade. The andean people are very good builders. They make their own homes, roads and irrigation systems, often using ancestral techniques.

A very few native groups, such as the *Cayapas (Chachis)*, *Sáchilas*, and *Cuaiqueros* continue to lead a traditional lifestyle on the Pacific coast. In the Amazon basin, traditional life among its native peoples is also increasingly scarce and is based on hunting, fishing, gathering and small scale farming.

Among the *mestizos* two sub-groups can be identified: that resulting from the mixing of the native indian races and european immigrants, and that resulting from the mixing of peoples of european and african descent. The former is more noticeable in the highlands, whereas the latter can be seen more commonly along the Pacific coast and in certain highland valleys. The lifestyles of these two groups are distinct, due not only to differences in cultural heritage, but also to the differences in habitat. Meals among the highland *mestizos* center around pork, potatoes, corn, young grains and vegetables; whereas for those of the coast, fish, rice, plantain, mature grains and vegetables are the principal dietary staples.
Mestizos in general are very friendly. On festive occasions they tend to be very open and show their affection with big meals, drinking and dancing. There are frequent celebrations for the anniversary of the founding of a city or the cantonization of a region and for all religious occasions. Orchestras, brass and string bands, parades, bull fights, exhibitions and contests are generally a part of such celebrations.

A particularly colorful festivity throughout the country is that of New Year's Eve. On December 31, home-made life-size puppets called *años viejos* (the old year), depicting events from the year that is about to end, are put on display in front of private homes and public buildings. Children dress up as widows and ask for donations for their husband, the old year, who is dying. At midnight a will, describing the legacy of the outgoing year, is read and the *años viejos* are doused with gasoline and set ablaze, thus ending the year and all it had brought with it.

LANGUAGE

Spanish and *Quichua* are the official national languages. Spanish is spoken throughout almost all of Ecuador. *Quichua*, the ancient language of the Inca empire, is spoken by two million Ecuadorians in many andean and amazonian communities.

Other languages are also spoken by the tribal peoples of the Amazon basin. There are various linguistic institutes and many private schools providing ample opportunities for the interested visitor to study these tongues.

MUSIC

Ecuadorian music also reflects the varied cultural past of the country. The influence of ancient andean music is noticeable in the popular rhythms known as *San Juanito*, *Cachullapi*, *Albazo*, *Yumbo* and *Danzante*. The European influence can be noticed in the *Pasacalles* and *Pasillos*, which are also popular throughout the country. The xylophone and drum music of the province of Esmeraldas reflects the african roots of its inhabitants. In addition, the *Cumbia* and *Vallenato*, originally from Colombia, caribbean rhythms like *Salsa*, *Merengue* and *Son*, and a wide variety international music is currently played throughout Ecuador.

FOOD

Like almost everything else in Ecuador, the cuisine varies extensively with region. The following are some typical dishes worth trying.

In the highlands: *locro de papas* (potato and cheese soup), *mote* (corn burst with alkali), *caldo de patas* (soup made with pigs knuckles and mote), *llapingachos* (potato and cheese patties), *empanadas de morocho* (fried snacks of ground corn dough filled with meat), *sancocho de yuca* (vegetable soup with manioc root), roast *cuy* (guinea pig), *fritada* (fried pork), *hornado* (roast pork), *humitas* (tender ground corn steamed in the corn leaves), and *quimbolitos* (similar to humitas but prepared with corn flour and steamed in banana leaves). *Humitas* and *quimbolitos* come in both sweet and savory varieties.

On the coast: *empanadas de verde* (fried snacks of ground plantain dough, filled with cheese, meat or shrimp) *sopa de bolas de verde* (plantain dumpling soup), *ceviche* (marinated fish or seafood cocktail), *encocadas* (dishes prepared with coconut milk, may be shrimp, fish, etc.), *cocadas* (sweets made with coconut), *viche* (fish or seafood soup), *patacones* (thick fried plantain chips served as a side dish).

In the Amazon basin: dishes prepared with *yuca* (manioc or cassava root) and wide variety of river fish.

Ceviche has recently acquired a sinister reputation as one of the means of transmission of Cholera. In fact, only *ceviche de pescado* (fish) and *ceviche de concha* (oyster) which are marinated uncooked pose this hazard. The other varieties of *ceviche* such as *camarón* (shrimp), *langostino* (jumbo shrimp), and *langosta* (lobster), all of which are cooked before being marinated, are generally safe delicacies.

Ecuadorian food is not particularly spicy. However, in most homes and restaurants, the meal is accompanied by a small bowl of *ají* (hot red pepper sauce) which varies greatly in potency. Those unfamiliar with this condiment are advised to go easy at first.
In addition to the prepared foods mentioned above, Ecuador offers large variety of delicious temperate and tropical fruits, some of which are unique to South America.

PUBLIC SAFETY AND CONDUCT

In general, one is struck by the good will and hospitality of all Ecuadorians. None the less, common sense is essential in guiding a visitor's conduct as crime and hostility do exist here, just as they unfortunately exist everywhere else in the world. One simple precaution is to avoid the ostentatious display of one's wealth in the form of fancy camera equipment, jewelry, large wads of bills, etc. But despite a recent increase in violent crime in the largest cities, Ecuador as a whole remains among the safest and most relaxed countries on the entire South American continent.

In addition to looking out for one's own safety, the conscientious guest in this generous land has the obligation to treat his hosts with respect and courtesy. Ecuador and its people have much to offer the visitor and the visitor should be willing to offer something of himself (beyond mere financial compensation) in return. An effort to speak the local language, no matter how rudimentary, is always appreciated for example; as are good manners and discretion in the use of one's camera. Above all one must remember that it is the polite guest, in a country no less than in a private home, who is obliged to learn from and adapt to the ways of his hosts, rather than expecting that his own customs should prevail.

DRESS

Despite its tropical location, Ecuador's varied climate calls for more than shorts and a T-shirt. In the highlands, where cool damp weather is not unusual and the nights are always chilly, a warm sweater and rain gear are essential. Furthermore the conservative and somewhat formal customs of this part of the country should be taken into consideration. A jacket and tie are essential for business meetings and most official functions. Slacks, however, are perfectly acceptable for women. Although increasingly common, shorts are still looked at askance in many parts of the highlands (except for sports), and are certainly inappropriate for visiting churches and religious shrines. In the coastal and Amazon lowlands, both climate and custom dictate much lighter and less formal attire. The *guayabera*, a pleated light cotton men's short sleeved shirt, is suitable for almost all occasions.

HEALTH

Although a routine tourist's visit to Ecuador does not pose any serious hazards to one's health, the prudent traveler might consider certain precautions appropriate to the specific areas in which he plans to stay. Bottled mineral water is available throughout the country and is recommended in preference to tap water. Uncooked vegetables, especially lettuce, might be avoided by those unaccustomed to the local bacterial flora. Those visiting the highlands should take into account that they will require 24 to 48 hours to become acclimatized to the altitude, and should not undertake strenuous physical activity immediately upon arrival. Yellow Fever vaccination and Malaria prophylaxis are recommended for visitors to the Amazon jungle and the northern Pacific coast. Typhoid Fever vaccination, Cholera vaccination, and gamma globulin to prevent Hepatitis A, might be considered by those planning an extended visit or traveling independently outside the usual tourist areas. One should avoid walking barefoot on soil where swine are roaming loose as Trichinosis is endemic throughout the country. Precautions against sunburn are very important, especially at higher altitudes.

Good medical facilities are available in the major cities, although these may be expensive. The following are some of the better known private hospitals and clinics:

In Quito:

Hospital Metropolitano
Address: Mariana de Jesús.
Phone: 431-520
Centro Médico Quirúrgico Pichincha
Address: Veintimilla 1259 and Páez.
Phone: 562-408
Clínica Pasteur
Address: Eloy Alfaro 552 and Italia.
Phone: 546-519
Hospital Voz Andes
Address: Villalengua 267.
Phone: 252-142

In Guayaquil:

Hospital Luis Vernaza (Pensionado)
Address: J. Coronel 404 and Escobedo.
Phone: 560-300
Hospital Clínica Kennedy
Address: San Jorge and La Novena y Décima.
Phone: 286-963
Clínica Alcívar
Address: Coronel corner Azuay.
Phone: 444-287

In Cuenca:

Clínica Santa Inés
Address: Daniel Córdova Toral.
Phone: 817-888

Most of the above hospitals provide ambulance transportation. In addition, intensive care ambulance service in Quito is available from **Hospital Metropolitano** (phone: 431-520) and from **UTIM** (phone: 562-613). Intensive care air-ambulance service throughout the country, with international transfer capabilities, is available from **Ambulancias Aereas del Ecuador** (Quito phone: 449-191 - Dr. Cousen).

TOURIST FACILITIES

A wide variety of facilities are available ranging from luxurious hotels, gourmet restaurants, and five star resorts; to modest family run accommodations and eating establishments. Therefore there ought to be something to suit virtually every taste and budget. The national tourist agency CETUR (Corporación Ecuatoriana de Turismo), with its head office in Quito (Eloy Alfaro corner Carlos Tobar) and regional offices in other cities, provides maps and information for visitors.

TIPPING

Is customary in the more expensive hotels, restaurants and service establishments. Approximately 10% of the bill is appropriate for waiters and waitresses, a small tip of about US $0.50 for most other services.

LEGEND

Mayor city	
Province capital	
Regions main center	
Parish main center	
Paved road	
Unpaved road	
Railway	
Railway station	
International airport	
National airport	
Landing strip	
Commercial harbor	
International border	
Province border line	
Undefined province border	
Province's name	AZUAY
Lake	
River	
Relief map	

LEGEND

Native community

Indian fair

Archeological center

Grafts center

Historical site

Ruins

Religious shrine

Thermal baths

Beach

Sport fishing

Picturesque road

Protected area

Zoo

Grot / cave

Waterfall

High barren land

Snow capped mountain

Volcano

Original map: I.G.M.

Quito and the Northern Highlands

QUITO AND THE NORTHERN HIGHLANDS

The northern highlands of Ecuador, known as the *Sierra Norte*, extend from the Colombian border, at 1° north latitude, to the *Nudo del Azuay* a mountain ridge running east-west at 2°30' south latitude. The main urban center in this region is the city of Quito. It is located in an intermont basin, at the foot of Pichincha, a massive volcano whose highest of several peaks rises to 4.794 m. (15.724 ft.) above sea level.

SAN FRANCISCO DE QUITO

LOCATION AND GEOGRAPHY

Due to its position in a narrow valley running north-south, the city has grown longitudinally and now measures 30 km. (18,6 mi.) in length by only 3 to 5 km. (1,9 to 3,1 mi.) in width. Hence, present day Quito is confined to a long, narrow strip of land, wedged between the slopes of Pichincha to the west and an abrupt canyon formed by the river Machángara to the east. Across this canyon is a small mountain ridge, oriented N-S, rising approximately 300 m. (985 ft.) above the city, and beyond it spreads a much larger valley known as *Valle de los Chillos*, which is beginning to take up some of the city's newest growth. A small volcano, Ilaló, sits in the center of this valley. The city proper today covers an area of 12.000 Hectares (46,5 $mi.^2$) and the metropolitan area some 200.000 Hectares (772 $mi.^2$).

HISTORY AND DEVELOPMENT

In the pre-Inca era, the northern highlands were inhabited by several tribes, the most important of which were the *Caras* who lived in the north of the region, the *Quitus* in the central area and the *Puruháes* in the south.
The entire area came under the dominion of the Incas by the beginning of the 16th century, and Quito subsequently became the capital of the northern half of the *Tahuantinsuyo*, as the Inca empire was known.
Following the Spanish conquest, Quito and the northern highlands became the nucleus of the Crown Colony known as the *Real Audiencia de Quito*. The Spanish colonial city of Quito was founded on December 6, 1534, by the *conquistador* Sebastián de Benalcázar. It was built on the ruins of the ancient city of Quito, seat of government of *Atahualpa*, the last Inca ruler. His general, *Rumiñahui*, razed the city prior to the conquerors' arrival so that it wouldn't fall into foreign hands. The Spaniards completed the ancient city's destruction by using the rubble for their buildings. Even today one can find typical Inca stonework in the façades and floors of colonial buildings such as the Cathedral, the Church of San Francisco and some private homes.

Upon their arrival the Spaniards proceeded to divide the city of Quito into 200 lots, one for each *conquistador*. They used traditional Spanish urban planning practices placing a main square (*plaza central*) in the center of the city and projecting the streets around it.

The area's importance continued throughout the colonial period and when the Republic of Ecuador was created, Quito became its capital. At the same time the northern highlands were divided into the provinces of **Carchi** (capital: Tulcán), **Imbabura** (Ibarra), **Pichincha** (Quito), **Cotopaxi** (Latacunga), **Tungurahua** (Ambato), **Chimborazo** (Riobamba), and **Bolívar** (Guaranda), from north to south respectively. The names given to all of these provinces except for Carchi and Bolívar correspond to the name of the most prominent volcano in each region.

The current layout of the old city of Quito dates back to the end of the 1700s. Naturally, there have been some changes over the centuries. For example, the current Government Palace (*Palacio de Gobierno*) was not part of the original city. Private homes which occupied that location where bought out by the King's treasury in order to build the residence of the president of the Crown Colony.
The *Plaza Grande* (main square) and its surrounding buildings: the Government Palace, City Hall, Bishop's Residence and the Cathedral constitute the heart of colonial Quito.

The Government Palace was built by Carondelet, president of the Crown Colony towards the end of the 18th century, while the Cathedral dates to the end of the 16th century and was built by Quito's first bishop. Most of Quito's grandiose churches and convents were built during the colonial period. Every year something new was added: a new façade, a new gold altar, a new sculpture, painting or ornament, which enhanced the city's beauty.

EVOLUTION OF THE MODERN CITY

The 100th anniversary of Ecuador's independence in 1922, also marked the beginning of a new era in Quito's growth and a change in its urban style. An Uruguayan developer, Jones Odriozola, laid out the development plan for the northern part of the city in 1941. The 1950s saw the rise of a number of working class neighborhoods such as *La Ferroviaria* and *La Villaflora* in the south and *La Vicentina* and *Belisario Quevedo* in the north of the city. This growth towards both the north and south continued in the 1960s and peaked in the 1970s when the income from oil exports fueled the creation of numerous new upper, middle and working class neighborhoods in all areas of the city. The city continues to grow and a number of towns which were separate from the city in the past, are today part of the metropolitan area.

The climate in Quito varies with location. It is more humid in the south and drier in the north. The mean temperature is approximately 13°C (55°F). The temperature during the day is pleasant, generally reaching a high of 22°C (72°F) at midday and dropping in the afternoon and evening to a mean nighttime temperature of 11°C (52°F). During the winter (October to May), it often rains in the afternoon, but it is not unusual for the sky to clear in the evening, allowing the last rays of sun to shed their light over the mountains as the sun sets.

In addition to being the nation's capital, Quito is an important center of commerce, industry and higher education. It is home of three major universities and several polytechnic institutes.

QUITO'S MAIN COLONIAL BUILDINGS

(See the Colonial City Map for locations)

CHURCHES

The Cathedral: Quito's Cathedral was built in classical orthodox style. It is one of the first churches built in South America in the 16th century, however its portal and tower were only completed in the 20th century. Some fine examples of the works of the Quito School of Art can be seen in the interior chapels. The remains of the independence hero, Marshal Antonio José de Sucre, are kept in a small, simple chapel inside the Cathedral.

El Sagrario: Spanish tradition dictates the construction of this chapel. Built and decorated in the 17th century, its inner doors are gold plated and built in chiriguresque style. The main altar and the interior of the dome are particularly remarkable.

La Compañía: Built in the 18th century, La Compañía is one of the richest and most beautiful churches in Quito. Its façade carved in stone and its wooden interior covered in gold are definitely worth seeing. This church boasts some fine samples of the Quito School of Art, in particular Goríbar's paintings of the Prophets which can be seen on the columns of the central nave. The remains of the first Ecuadorian saint, Santa Mariana de Jesus, are kept on the main altar. The back of the church leads to what was once the famous Jesuit School of San Luis.

San Francisco: Construction on this very impressive church, a replica of the church of the Escorial Palace in Spain, started as soon as the city of Quito was founded in 1534. A number of colonial sculptures and paintings can be admired in its interior. Perhaps the best known of its paintings is *La Virgen de Quito* by Legarda, which depicts the Virgin Mary with silver wings. A large sculpture, based on this painting, is to be found atop the hill of *El Panecillo*, standing vigil over colonial Quito. The inner walls and ceiling of this church are exquisitely decorated. It has a very interesting adjoining convent with numerous examples of painting and sculpture by artists of the Quito School of Art. **The Chapel of Cantuña**, located next to the convent, has very beautiful sculptures which should not be missed. The *Plaza de San Francisco*, located directly in front of the church can be considered one of Quito's most important squares, as for over 400 years it has been the nucleus of the city's historical and political events.

Santo Domingo: This church and its adjoining convent were built towards the beginning of the Spanish colonial period. It is well known for its School of San Fernando which was created to teach philosophy and Latin. Paintings by Padre Bedón can be seen in this church.

San Agustín: This church and convent where built towards the end of the 16th century. Most interesting are its stone façade and the paintings in the convent by Miguel de Santiago (17th century). A cloister in this church known as la *Sala Capitular de San Agustín*, where the first act of independence from Spain was signed, is a national shrine for Ecuadorians and a place of pilgrimage. The convent of San Agustín was once the home of the *Universidad de San Fulgencio*, Quito's first university, founded in the 16th century.

La Merced: Construction on this church, built in baroque and moorish style, started at the beginning of the 17th century. It was built to commemorate Pichincha's eruptions which threatened to destroy the city. General Sucre and his soldiers prayed in this church for the wellbeing of the nation, following the decisive battle which gave Ecuador its independence in 1822. A visit to its cloister, library and fountain in the main patio, should not be missed.

OTHER COLONIAL STRUCTURES

Palacio de Gobierno: The Government Palace, which includes the seat of government and the president's official residence, is located on the west side of the main square, known as *Plaza de la Independencia* or *Plaza Grande*. It was built by Carondelet towards the end of the 18th century.

Arco de la Reina: The "Queen's Arch" was Quito's southern gate. It was built by Dionisio de Alcedo in the middle of the 18th century. A second arch built at that time was the "Arch of the Chapel of El Rosario", located next to the church of Santo Domingo.

Cuartel Real: Spanish barracks where, in 1810, the leaders of the first uprising against the monarchy, were executed. It houses a small museum which commemorates this historic event.

The Bishop's Palace: Headquarters of the religious authority and the bishop's official residence since the 16th century. It has been restored, and today part of it houses shops.

San Juan de Dios Hospital: One of the earliest buildings in Quito, it dates from the 16th century. Its sunny cloisters are very pleasant. The building has been renovated and today houses the Museum of Medicine.

MUSEUMS

Many of these museums can provide English or French speaking guides. Call well ahead to make the necessary arrangements.

Archeological Museum of the Central Bank:
Address: Casa de la Cultura Ecuatoriana
Phone: 223-259
This museum, run by the Central Bank of Ecuador, has the most complete and best organized archeological collection in the country. It presents a complete historical review of Ecuadorian civilization, from the pre-ceramic era (4000 B.C.) until the Inca civilization (1533 A.D.). Beautiful ceramics and gold pieces are on display, including a stunning gold mask, possibly representing the sun god. A visit here is highly recommended. The Central Bank also has a fine collection of colonial and religious art which will be moved to the Casa de la Cultura Ecuatoriana by mid to late 1992.

Hours: Tuesday to Friday: 9:00 - 17:00 hrs.
Saturday & Sunday: 10:00 - 15:00 hrs.

National Museum of Colonial Art:
Address: Cuenca corner Mejía.
Phone: 212-297
Housed in the 17th century house of the Marqués de Villacís, this museum has a fine collection of paintings, sculptures and ceramics from the Quito School of Art. In this collection you can find masterpieces by well known artists such as Miguel de Santiago, Bernardo Rodríguez, Manuel Samaniego, Bernardo de Legarda and Caspicara.

Hours: Tuesday to Friday: 10:00 - 18:00 hrs.
Saturday: 10:00 - 14:00 hrs.

Museum of the Convent of San Francisco:
Address: Cuenca 477, Plaza de San Francisco.
Phone & fax: 581-281
The access to this museum is through the main cloister of the San Francisco Convent. It houses a large and very valuable collection of artwork which has been accumulated through the centuries of the convent's existence. Very old works from artists of the Quito School of Art, such as

Miguel de Santiago, Goríbar, Rodríguez and Mejía, are on display. It also has a collection of twenty-two 18th century paintings on marble and many examples of crafts.

Hours: Monday to Saturday: 9:00 - 18:00 hrs.
Sunday: 9:00 - 13:00 hrs.

"Fray Pedro Bedón" Dominican Museum:
Address: Flores 150, Plaza de Santo Domingo.
Phone: 210-723
Religious Art museum with a large collection of colonial art. Among its most valuable pieces are: the collection known as "The Kings of Israel" by Nicolás J. Goríbar, paintings and cover plates by Fray Pedro Bedón, sculptures by Legarda, "The Virgin" of the Nativity by Caspicara, "Saint Joseph the Mountain Man", 39 bas-reliefs by the Spanish artist Diego de Robles and the "Throne of the Virgin", a silver piece weighing 363 kg. (800 pounds).

Hours: Monday to Friday: 9:00-12:30 & 14:00-16:30 hrs.
Saturday & Sunday: 9:00 - 16:00 hrs.

"Jijón y Caamaño" Museum:
Address: Catholic University of Quito, 12 de Octubre, Main Library Building, 3rd. floor.
Phone: 529-250 ext. 1317
This fine museum has two sections. The first, of colonial art, has a collection of ceramics, as well as prime samples of the works by Quito's artists such as Mateo Mejía, Miguel de Santiago, Goríbar, Antonio Salas, Juan Manosalvas and Joaquín Pinto. The second, houses the collection of the renowned Ecuadorian archeologist, Jacinto Jijón y Caamaño, founder of the museum. These pieces were gathered over his lifetime of exploration in the Andes of Ecuador and Perú.

Hours: Monday to Friday: 9:00 - 16:00 hrs.

"Weilbauer - Porras" Museum:
Address: Catholic University of Quito, 12 de Octubre corner Ladrón de Guevara.
Phone: 230-577
Run by the Center for Archeological Studies of the University, this museum presents archeological pieces from all the regions of Ecuador.

Hours: Monday to Friday: 9:00-13:00 & 14:00-16:00 hrs.

"Camilo Egas" Museum: Fundación Cinco
Address: Venezuela 1302 and Esmeraldas.
Phone: 514-511
This museum, run by the Fundación Cinco, houses a collection of paintings representative of all the works of the Ecuadorian artist Camilo Egas (1889-1962).

Hours: Monday to Friday: 9:00-12:00 & 15:00-18:00 hrs.
Saturday: 9:00 - 18:00 hrs.

Museums of the Casa de la Cultura Ecuatoriana:
Address: 12 de Octubre and Patria.
Phone: 223-392
The Casa de la Cultura Ecuatoriana is a national institution founded in 1944 with the aim of preserving and spreading Ecuadorian culture. It operates several museums, three of which are located in its national headquarters. The **Museum of Art** exhibits works of the republican era, starting in 1830. It houses prime works of the most renowned painters of the 19th century and painters and sculptors of the 20th century. The **Museum of Ethnology** has a fine display of Ecuadorian culture, identifying different ethnic groups by their dress, work, pottery and masks. The **Museum of Musical Instruments** has a very complete and impressive display of American and European instruments from the collection of the artist Pedro Traversari. The **Museum of Colonial and Religious Art** of the Central Bank will be added to this cultural center by mid to late 1992.

Hours: Tuesday to Friday: 10:00 - 18:00 hrs.
Saturday: 10:00 - 14:00 hrs.

Ecuadorian Museum of Natural Sciences:
Address: Rumipamba 341 and De los Shyris Av.
(La Carolina Park).
Phone: 449-824
This natural history museum, operated by the Casa de la Cultura Ecuatoriana, displays a well classified and documented collection of Ecuadorian flora and fauna.

Hours: Monday to Friday: 8:30-13:00 & 14:00-16:30 hrs.
Saturday: 9:00 - 13:00 hrs.
Sunday: 9:30 - 14:30 hrs.

Guayasamín Museum:
Address: José Bosmediano 543.
Phone: 446-455
Private collection owned by the renowned Ecuadorian painter Oswaldo Guayasamín, who has exhibited his art throughout Europe and the Americas. The museum has select works of Ecuadorian art, especially from the colonial period. This museum doubles as an art studio where special design jewelry and other artifacts are crafted.

Hours: Monday to Friday: 9:30-13:00 & 15:00-18:30 hrs.
Saturday: 9:30 - 13:00 hrs.

"Casa de Sucre" Historical Museum:
Address: Venezuela corner Sucre.
Phone: 512-860
This museum is located in the beautiful colonial house which belonged to Marshal Antonio José de Sucre.

It is administered by the Ministry of National Defense and it has a collection of arms, clothing, furniture and documents related to this hero of the struggle for independence from Spain.

Hours: Tuesday to Friday: 8:30-12:00 & 13:30-16:00 hrs.
Saturday: 8:30 - 13:00 hrs.

"La Cima de la Libertad" Military Museum:
Address: De los Libertadores Av.
This museum and National Monument, built and operated by the Ministry of National Defence is located on the slopes of the Pichincha Volcano, on the exact spot where the pro-independence forces won the decisive Battle of Pichincha on May 24, 1822. It contains various artifacts related to the struggle for independence and an eternal flame to remember those fallen in battle.

Hours: Tuesday to Friday: 8:30 - 16:00 hrs.
Saturday: 10:00 - 14:00 hrs.

SHOPPING CENTERS

Caracol:
Address: Amazonas and Naciones Unidas.
Phone: 458-553

Centro Comercial Iñaquito (C.C.I.):
Address: Amazonas and Naciones Unidas.
Phone: 259-444

El Bosque:
Address: Occidental and E. Carvajal.
Phone: 456-333

El Espiral:
Address: J. Washington.
Phone: 566-221

El Recreo:
Address: Pedro Vicente Maldonado.
(Trolebus last station - Estación Sur)
Phone: 666-501

Mall El Jardín:
Address: República corner Amazonas.
Phone: 980-298

Multicentro:
Address: 6 de Diciembre and La Niña.
Phone: 237-949

Naciones Unidas (C.C.N.U.):
Address: Naciones Unidas and Japón.
Phone: 459-094

Quicentro:
Address: Naciones Unidas and 6 de Diciembre.
Phone: 464-526

Unicornio:
Address: Amazonas and Naciones Unidas.

MARKETS

Produce markets throughout Ecuador are very colorful and definitely merit a visit, especially for those who care to see and sample the many exotic fruits that grow here. Beware of pickpockets and make sure to wash the produce very well before eating it. The following are some of Quito's principal markets:

Santa Clara:
Address: Versalles and Marchena.

Mercado Central:
Address: Pichincha and Esmeraldas.

Iñaquito:
Address: Amazonas and Villalengua.

HANDICRAFTS

Amazonas avenue and the colonial center. Beautiful handicrafts made throughout Ecuador can be found in Quito. A large number of craft shops are concentrated into two locations in the city. Amazonas Av. between Patria Av. and Colón Av. and all the nearby cross-streets have many sidewalk stalls in addition to craft shops. In the colonial center, craft shops are found at the base of the Government Palace and also on Guayaquil street, one of the main commercial streets in downtown Quito. Bargaining is the norm in the street, in marketplaces, in many smaller commercial establishments and most craft shops. A few of the cooperatives however, do have genuine set prices. A few of the larger crafts shops, which have a wide selection of merchandise are listed below.

OCEPA:
Address [1]: Carrión 1236 and Versalles.
Phone: 227-421
Address [2]: Jorge Washington 252 and Amazonas.
Phone: 236-334
Address [3]: Amazonas 2615 and La Granja.
Phone: 449-671

Productos Andinos (Craftsmen's Cooperative):
Address: Urbina 111 and Luis Cordero.
Phone: 224-565

Almacén de Artesanías Ecuador:
Address: Amazonas 232 and 18 de Septiembre.
Phone: 523-615

Folklore Olga Fisch (Exclusive Designs):
Address [1]: Colón 260 and J. Caamaño.
Phone: 563-085
Address [2]: Oro Verde Hotel
Address [3]: Colón Hotel

PLACES OF INTEREST NEAR QUITO

The Equator: The equator, known as *La Línea Equinoccial* or *La Mitad del Mundo*, is an imaginary line which divides the Planet Earth into two equal parts: the northern and southern hemispheres. This line passes just a few kilometers north of Quito, by the town of San Antonio de Pichincha, and a monument marks its exact location. This monument was erected to acknowledge the accomplishments of the Geodetic Mission which came to Ecuador to study the shape of the earth between 1736 and 1742. The 30 m. (98 ft.) high, volcanic rock, pyramidal monument has an anthropological museum in its interior.
In an avenue leading to the monument stand the busts of the scientists who participated in this important mission: 9 members of the Academy of Science in Paris, 2 Spanish mathematicians and the Ecuadorian scientist Pedro Vicente Maldonado. Next to the monument there is an exhibition hall, where Ecuador, France, Spain and Germany have pavilions displaying scientific and historical exhibits related to the 18th century scientific mission and its accomplishments.
Nearby, the Provincial Government has built a Spanish colonial village showing typical urban architecture of the time, such as the central *plaza*, church, bull fight ring and city hall. The village houses gift shops, restaurants, a planetarium and a scale model of colonial Quito.

The Crater of Pululahua: Pululahua, a dormant volcano, is located just a few kilometers from the monument to the equator. Its crater is a giant cauldron which has, over the years, been partially filled by sedimentation. This crater is home to a number of farmers, their flocks and fertile fields. The peaceful lives they lead stand in striking contrast to the violent volcanic past of their surroundings. The paved road leads to the windy eastern rim, from where you can look down into the crater. Those feeling fit, can walk down along a dirt path and admire the changing vegetation with the change in altitude. The very bottom has its own micro-climate. It is about a 45 minute walk down, 90 minutes back up, and well worth the effort. Pululahua is but one of many volcanic cauldrons which can be found in the northern Ecuadorian Andes, it has recently been declared a National Geo-botanical Reserve.

The Inca Ruins of Rumicucho: These Inca ruins are located 3 km. from San Antonio de Pichincha, also not far from the monument to the equator. They are in rather poor condition after many years of neglect, but this site has been useful in the study of the conquest of the northern Andes by the Incas, towards the end of their reign.

The most outstanding aspects of this site are its strategic location and commanding view. The ruins sit atop a small elongated hill, above a deep canyon, overlooking the Puéllaro valley and the Guayllabamba river to the north. The view is breathtaking.

Cochasquí: A pre-Inca archeological site composed of a dozen pyramids and several smaller burial mounds, located 47 km. (29 mi.) north of Quito. The pyramids, which are made of a hardened clay known as *cangagua*, give the impression of being an intrinsic part of the hill on which they were built. They have been extensively studied by archeologists, and it is felt that they are the remains of an important political and ceremonial center dating back to approximately 900 AD. Access to the site is by a dirt road going north off the Guayllabamba-Tabacundo road, 8 km. (5 miles) west of Tabacundo. A small sign reading *"Tolas de Cochasquí"* marks the access road.

Calderón: The town of Calderón lies just north of Quito, along the Panamerican Highway. It is famous for its figurines and dolls made of bread-dough. A large number of shops offer the visitor a wide selection of these and other handicrafts as well as the opportunity to see the craftsmen at work.

Los Chillos Valley: In colonial times this large, fertile valley, east of Quito, was the site of the large *haciendas* owned by the nobility and clergy. Today it looks like a patchwork quilt. Small farms are interspersed with suburban residential neighborhoods, country homes, a few industrial installations and some large, old farms, still owned by Quito's traditional noble families. Due to the valley's mild climate and the thermal baths located in Tingo, Alangasí and La Merced, Los Chillos is a favorite destination for weekend family outings.

Ilaló: A volcanic cone, with an eroded crater sits in the middle of the valley, and deep river canyons follow their course towards the north. To the south lies the **Pasochoa Volcano**, which in recent years was declared a national forest. It has a native, subtropical mountain forest, which is worth a visit. There are several good nature trails of varying lengths and camping is permitted. Access to the park is via a cobbled road leading east, off the main Sangolquí-Tambillo road, just south of the turnoff to Amaguaña. It is marked by a small green sign reading: *"Bosque Protector Pasochoa"*.

Papallacta Thermal Baths: A second road heading east from Quito, leads to the Tumbaco, Cumbayá valley, another weekend outing favorite among *quiteños*. Beyond this valley, along the road to Baeza in the Ecuadorian Amazon, are the thermal baths of Papallacta, located 80 km. (50 mi.) east of Quito. The road is paved until the pass on the central range of the Andes and is in very good condition for the remainder. These baths are in a particularly beautiful setting, surrounded by mountains covered in rain forest.

PROVINCES OF THE NORTHERN HIGHLANDS

CARCHI

Tulcán: The capital of this northernmost province of the highlands is a busy commercial center. The **Tulcán Cemetery** is adorned with cypress trees carved into living sculptures representing pre-columbian mythical figures. The sculptures are extremely well done and are worth a visit. To the west of Tulcán are the **Tufiño medicinal thermal bath**, whose waters comes from the Chiles Volcano. The **Gruta de la Paz**, near the town of Bolívar, is a grotto with the figure of the "Virgin of Peace" among the stalactites and stalagmites. It is located in a beautifully lush setting. Between the towns of El Angel and San Isidro, lies the **Páramo del Angel**, were the unique velvet covered andean plant, the *frailejón* (great friar), can be admired.

IMBABURA

This province is known for its scenic lakes and its handicrafts.

San Antonio de Ibarra: A town just west of the provincial capital Ibarra, produces and sells beautiful wood carvings. West of the town of **Cotacachi**, where leather goods are sold, lies **Cuicocha**, a lake which fills a deep volcanic crater. The site is very beautiful and is part of the Cotacachi-Cayapas National Reserve. Boat rides can be taken on the lake, there is a walking trail which goes around the lake (4 to 6 hours) and camping is possible in the area. Two other scenic lakes in the province of Imbabura are **Yaguarcocha** and **San Pablo**.

Otavalo: After Quito, must be the place most visited by tourists in the ecuadorian highlands. This town, whose residents dress in traditional attire, is located about one and a half hours north of Quito. It is famous for its Saturday indian fair. One section of the fair (*Plaza de los Ponchos*) is devoted exclusively to textiles featuring a wide selection of woven and knitted handicrafts. There is ample selection but prices are not necessarily better than in the Quito craft shops. There are smaller fairs in Otavalo on Sundays and Wednesdays.

PICHINCHA

This large province, of which Quito is the capital, covers a variety of geographical areas, ranging from high andean peaks to subtropical lowlands. Pichincha has many dairy farms, located in the inter-andean basins, to the north and south of the capital city. The **Lagunas de Mojanda** are three lakes, located west of the Panamerican Highway, 15 km. (9 mi.) north of the town of **Cayambe**. The high moorland surroundings are very scenic.

Santo Domingo de los Colorados: Is a city located west of the Andes, at 300 m. (984 ft.) above sea level. It is Ecuador's main transportation hub connecting the highlands with the coast and the country's most rapidly growing urban center. Its main attractions are the lush scenery and its native people, popularly known as *Los Colorados* (the red people), although they call themselves the *Sáchila*. Their nickname was given because of their tradition of painting their bodies and coating their hair with *achiote* (annato), a red vegetable dye. Years ago, the *Colorados* were frequently seen on the streets of Santo Domingo in their traditional body paint and clothes. Today this is a rare sight. In order to visit the *Colorados*, one must go to the small villages where a few members of this ethnic group still maintain their traditions. Today, tourism is an important source of income for the *Colorados*, and they charge to have their picture taken. Their rapid assimilation and cultural disintegration is a sad example of the pernicious impact of the modern world, and unbridled tourist curiosity, on aboriginal peoples.

COTOPAXI

In addition to **Cotopaxi National Park** and the **El Boliche Recreation Area** (see national parks section), this province is known for its colorful fairs, such as the one in **Latacunga**, the capital, on Saturdays and in **Saquisilí** on Thursdays. The town of **Pujilí** produces very colorful ceramics. The Corpus Christi celebrations in Pujilí and Saquisilí are very picturesque and interesting. 75 km. (46,5 mi.) over mountain roads from Pujilí is **Quilotoa**, a volcanic cone with an emerald green lake in its crater.

TUNGURAHUA

Ambato: The capital of Tungurahua is an important commercial center, especially known for its shoe and leather goods industry. It is also the center of a rich agricultural area and it is therefore known as "the city of the fruits and flowers". Ambato's Carnival celebrations are very colorful and well attended.

Baños: Forty kilometers (25 mi.) southeast of Ambato, at the foot of the Tungurahua Volcano, lies this resort town. It is well known for its thermal baths and beautiful surroundings. A visit to the main church is recommended. Mount Tungurahua is popular with hikers and climbers. There are a number of spectacular waterfalls along the road leading east from Baños towards the Ecuadorian Amazon.

CHIMBORAZO

This province, located in the geographical center of the country is named for Ecuador's highest peak. **Chimborazo** is a spectacular massive snow-covered mountain standing 6.310 m. (20.697 ft.) above sea level. A visit to the cold *páramo* (high moorlands) that surround it reveals unique fauna and scenery. There are two shelters for climbers, the lower of which, can be reached by car, off the Ambato to Guaranda road, or from Riobamba via the town of San Juan. Chimborazo, the world's highest summit measured from the center of the earth, is a substantial mountaineering challenge.

Riobamba: The provincial capital has a very privileged location, surrounded by magnificent snow-capped volcanoes. From the *Loma de Quito*, a park in town, one can admire the beauty of Chimborazo, Carihuairazo, Tungurahua, El Altar and occasionally the plume of smoke and ash over Sangay. The town of **Guano**, 12 km. (7,4 mi.) north of Riobamba is known for its high quality, hand made woolen rugs. The province of Chimborazo has many native people who maintain the andean traditions and way of life.

BOLIVAR

This province, located west of Chimborazo, has an especially varied geography and scenery, since it extends from the highest peak of the Andes, down to the foothills on the coastal plain. On its high plains surrounding Mt. Chimborazo is the **Chimborazo Wildlife Reserve** (see national parks section). **Guaranda** the provincial capital is a very peaceful, pleasant town surrounded by hills. Its Carnival is very colorful. The town of **Salinas** to the north of Guaranda is renowned for its high quality cheeses. The road Ambato - Guaranda - San Miguel - Balzapamba - Babahoyo is a very scenic alternative to the Santo Domingo road, when traveling from the highlands to the coast.

Guayaquil and the Pacific Coast

GUAYAQUIL AND THE PACIFIC COAST

The Pacific coastal region of Ecuador is divided into the following five provinces from north to south: **Esmeraldas** (capital: Esmeraldas), **Manabí** (Portoviejo), **Los Rios** (Babahoyo), **Guayas** (Guayaquil) and **El Oro** (Machala).

SANTIAGO DE GUAYAQUIL

LOCATION AND GEOGRAPHY

Guayaquil is located on the western shore of the Guayas River, at the point were the latter is formed by the confluence of the Daule and the Babahoyo. These rivers drain most of Ecuador's coastal plain. To the west of the city lies a large tidal salt marsh: the *Estero Salado*. It penetrates deep inland and forms a network of interconnecting channels surrounding many islands, covered by low spiny brush and fringed by mangroves.

Guayaquil's climate is dry between June and September and quite humid throughout the rest of the year. The humidity may be extreme during the rainy season, January to May. Temperatures range between 18°C and 28°C (64°F - 82°F) in the dry months between 24°C and 32°C (75°F - 90°F) in the rainy season. Paradoxically, the hot and humid time of the year is called *invierno* (winter).

The city's elevation is only 4 m. (13 ft.) above sea level. It is surrounded by a flat plain with very poor drainage. To the west lie some low mountains, the southern edge of the coastal range. To the east are plantations, pasture land and woods.

HISTORY AND DEVELOPMENT

Guayaquil was founded on July 25, 1537, by Francisco de Orellana, by what had been important indigenous settlements of sailors and fishermen. The name of the city comes from the Huancavilca chief *Guayas* and his wife *Quil*. Legend has it that this couple took their lives so that they would not fall in the hands of the Spaniards.

This river and ocean port rapidly gained importance for the Spanish Empire, as a stopping point for its galleons that sailed the Pacific Ocean. The area around Guayaquil provided wood for the construction of ships, partly in Guayaquil, but mainly in El Callao, the colonies' main port, in Peru. Commercial ties between these two ports became very strong during the colonial period. Towards the end of the 16th century and during the 17th century, Guayaquil was sacked and burnt on several occasions by the pirates who roamed the southern seas, including the infamous Captain Morgan. Guayaquil grew in importance after Ecuador's independence from Spain. In addition to being the country's main port, it gradually became its most populous city and its most important economic and industrial center.

Guayaquil is the provincial capital of Guayas, Ecuador's most populous province and one of the most productive regions in the country. Sadly, it also has some of the worst poverty in Ecuador. *El Guasmo*, situated on the south side of Guayaquil, is a notorious slum. Crime is all too common in the city and visitors are advised to take special precautions with their valuables.

CHURCHES

The Cathedral:
Address: Chimborazo and Clemente Ballén.
Phone: 512-865
Construction on this beautiful gothic style cathedral started at the end of the 19th century and it was completed only a few years ago. Its altar is made of marble. This is Guayaquil's main church, where the Archbishop presides.

Santo Domingo:
Address: Rocafuerte and J. Coronel.
Phone: 563-569
One of the oldest churches in Guayaquil, it dates back to the 16th century. It was destroyed several times in Guayaquil's fires. Decorations in the interior are by the painter Salas.

La Merced:
Address: V.M. Rendón and Pedro Carbo.
Phone: 305-468
A modern church, built in gothic style. Its baroque altar is gold plated.

San Francisco:
Address: 9 de Octubre and Pedro Carbo.
Phone: 320-088
One of the first churches of Guayaquil. It suffered the same fate as others of its era, and was destroyed several times. It was rebuilt in gothic style.

MUSEUMS

Municipal Museum and Library:
Address: Sucre and Pedro Carbo.
Phone: 531-691
It has four sections: Archeology, History, Colonial Art and Modern Art.

Hours: Tues. to Saturday: 9:00-12:30 & 13:00-17:00 hrs.

Museum of the Casa de la Cultura:
Address: 9 de Octubre and Moncayo.
Phone: 300-586
Archeological museum which includes a fine collection of gold pieces. This cultural center also includes a theater and the schools of art, ballet, music and drama.

Hours: Tuesday to Friday: 10:00 - 17:30 hrs.
Saturday: 9:00 - 15:00 hrs.

Museum of the Universidad Estatal:
Address: Ciudadela Universitaria.
Phone: 294-091
Run by the Archeology and History Departments of the national university.

Hours: Monday to Friday: 8:00 - 15:00 hrs.

Central Bank Museum:
Address: Antepara and 9 de Octubre.
Phone: 323-466
Anthropology and Modern Art Museum, run by the Central Bank of Ecuador.

Hours: Tuesday to Friday: 10:00 - 18:00 hrs.
Saturday: 10:00 - 16:00 hrs.
Sunday: 10:00 - 14:00 hrs.

MONUMENTS

Monument to the Liberators:
Address: El Malecón (waterfront drive) and the base of 9 de Octubre.
This statue of Simón Bolívar and José de San Martín commemorates the meeting, which took place on July 26, 1822, between these two leaders of the South American struggle for independence from Spain.

Monument to the Heroes of Independence *(Próceres)*:
Address: Guayaquil's Plaza del Centenario, between 9 de Octubre and Pedro Moncayo.
This monument has 4 statues representing the following: history, justice, patriotism and heroism.

Monument to Sucre:
Address: Clemente Ballén, between el Malecón and Pichincha.
This is a monument to Antonio José de Sucre, hero of the Battle of Pichincha, which gave Ecuador its independence.

Monument to Olmedo:
Address: El Malecón and Olmedo.
It is a monument to José Joaquín Olmedo, a renowned poet and statesman, who was born in Guayaquil.

Monument to Simón Bolívar:
Address: Chimborazo and Clemente Ballén.
This bronze statue was sculpted in France, in honor of Simón Bolívar, leader of independence.

Monument to Guayas and Quil:
Statues in honor of the Chief of the Huancavilcas and his wife, after whom the city was named.

OTHER PLACES OF INTEREST

Centro Cívico: Located at the south end of the city, it is a complex with exhibition halls and convention centers. A modern statue about independence, by the artist Oswaldo Guayasamín, decorates this center.

Las Peñas Neighborhood: This quaint old neighborhood, on the shores of the River Guayas, is part of the original settlement of Guayaquil and dates back to the 16th century. It has narrow colonial streets and traditional homes.

SHOPPING CENTERS

Garzocentro
Address: Agustín Freire and Guillermo Pareja.
Phone: 241-300

Policentro:
Address: San Jorge, Nueva Kennedy.
Phone: 290-194

Plaza Mayor
Address: Guillermo Pareja.
Phone: 240-036

Riocentro
Address: Vía San Borondón, km. 1,5
Phone: 834-171

La Rotonda
Address: B. Carrión and Tercera.
Phone: 242-945

Unicentro:
Address: Aguirre and Chile.
Phone: 328-912

Complejo Comercial Albán Borja:
Address: C.J. Arosemena, km. 2,5
Phone: 201-458

Plaza Triángulo:
Address: V.E. Estrada and Dátiles, Urdesa.
Phone: 383-608

Las Vitrinas:
Address: Décima. and H Str., Nueva Kennedy.
Phone: 286-143

Albocentro:
Address: Alborada, III Etapa.

Plaza Quil:
Address: Carlos Luis Plaza Dañín.

Las Bahías: Downtown Guayaquil has a busy commercial area, known as *Las Bahías*, crammed with small shops and stands overflowing with merchandise at supposedly bargain prices. Some of the foreign products sold in these shops, are found only here, as they come directly from the ships anchored offshore. Be especially wary of thieves and pickpockets in this area.

PLACES OF INTEREST NEAR GUAYAQUIL

Salinas: This oceanside resort is located 150 km. (93 mi.) west of Guayaquil, near the tip of the Santa Elena Peninsula, continental Ecuador's westernmost point. It is a very popular vacation spot and it gets crowded during the school holidays (December to March for coastal dwellers, July to September for people from the highlands).
Salinas has grown rapidly in last two decades, and today it is a bustling resort town, filled with luxury high-rise apartment buildings. A number of water sports are available and it is Ecuador's main center for yachting and deep-sea sport fishing.
Although many people bathe in Salinas, caution is advised, because the ocean can be rough and it is less than clean. There are a number of nicer bathing beaches just north of Salinas, such as Olón and Montañita. Other places worth visiting in the area are Punta Carnero and Ancón, also known as La Puntilla.

Playas: Also known as General Villamil, is an oceanside resort, located 90 km. (56 mi.) southwest of Guayaquil. It is a popular resort because of its long beaches and calm surf. Playas is a fishing village and its friendly inhabitants can still be seen coming in with the catch of the day in their traditional balsa rafts, with one large white sail.
The road ends southeast of Playas, at Posorja, a small fishing port located in the Gulf of Guayaquil. The scenery and the beaches between these two towns are very pretty.

PROVINCES OF THE PACIFIC COAST

ESMERALDAS

This is the northernmost of Ecuador's coastal provinces, and its capital city, also called **Esmeraldas**, is one of the country's four deep-sea ports. Esmeraldas is home to most of Ecuador's small black population, the descendants of slaves shipwrecked along the pacific coast or brought in to work the sugar cane fields during colonial times. The African cultural influence can be felt today in both the regional music and cooking.
The coastline of Esmeraldas is by far the lushest in Ecuador, with many islets and mangrove swamps in the far north, and palm fringed beaches further south. The surf along this coastline tends to be much warmer than in provinces to the south.

The most popular bathing beaches are to be found near the towns of **Atacames**, **Súa**, **Same**, and **Muisne**, all south of the city of Esmeraldas.

There is a fascinating, though very strenuous, train trip from **Ibarra**, in the highlands, to the northern outpost town of **San Lorenzo**, on the coast by the Colombian border. Crowding, long delays, and equipment failure are common, but the voyage takes one from the high *cordillera* through steep valleys to pristine coastal rainforests and offers unsurpassed scenery along the way. Detailed local inquiry is recommended before embarking as conditions on this route are constantly changing.
There are no road connections to San Lorenzo, but one may return to Quito by airplane, or proceed south along the coast by launch to the roadhead at **La Tola**, which has bus connections to the provincial capital. This too is a demanding but rewarding voyage.

MANABI

This province lies to the south of Esmeraldas and has its capital in **Portoviejo**, an important regional center of commerce and industry. Thirty-four km. (21 mi.) to the west is the city of **Manta**, also commercially important, and Ecuador's second port after Guayaquil.

The province's coastline boasts many fine beaches, and a gradual progression from lush to arid scenery is observed as one travels from north to south. **Bahía de Caráquez** and nearby **San Vicente** are resort towns with access to spectacular, broad, white sand beaches and delightful surf. The stretch of virgin beach between **San Vicente** and the village of **Canoa** is perhaps the finest in all of Ecuador. Other good beach areas are to be found near the towns of **Pedernales**, **San Clemente**, **San Jacinto**, **Crucita**, **Puerto Cayo**, and **Salango**.
There are roads all along Manabí's extensive shoreline but only the section from Puerto Cayo south is paved. The others are generally easily transitable during the dry season but may require a four-wheel-drive vehicle or be totally impassable during heavy rains. Local inquiry is advised. **Machalilla National Park** is located along Manabí's coastline (see National Parks section for details).

The town of **Montecristi**, situated 11 km. (7 mi.) inland from Manta, is known for its *sombreros de paja toquilla* (Panama hats) woven out of fine straw. Their quality was so renowned that the very best such hats came to be refered to as *Montecristi finos*, although this has now been adopted as a trade name by a commercial enterprise. Relatively few hats are still woven in the town itself, but there remains much commercial activity centered around their finishing, sale, and export. Hat prices are much better here than in Quito, and other handicrafts are also available.

LOS RIOS

This province is located inland along the Pacific coastal plain and has its capital in **Babahoyo**. It is one of Ecuador's foremost agricultural regions, producing much of the country's rice and bananas. Los Ríos was the home of several important pre-columbian cultures such as the *Chorrera*, *Valdivia*, *Tejar-Daule* and *Milagro-Quevedo* groups.

GUAYAS

This is Ecuador's most populous and most productive province. It is described under the preceding section on **Guayaquil**, its capital.

EL ORO

This is the southernmost of Ecuador's coastal provinces, bordering on Peru. It's capital is the city of **Machala**. Banana production for export is the province's most important industry and most of Ecuador's banana crop is shipped through the port of **Puerto Bolívar** near Machala. As the province's name suggests, gold mining also takes place here.

Also near Machala, with boat access from the old wharf in Puerto Bolívar, is the small island of **Jambelí** known for its calm ocean beach. Visitors should be sure to protect themselves against sunburn here as there is very little shade.

TOURIST MAP OF GUAYAQUIL

MUSEUMS

1	Antropológico y Arte Moderno del Banco Central	C-3
2	Arqueológico Banco del Pacífico	D-3
3	Arqueológico Casa de la Cultura	C-3
4	Del Municipio	C-3
5	Francisco Campos	B-4
6	Histórico BAE Calderón	C-1
7	Nahím Isaías Barquet	D-3
8	Naval Almirante Juan Illingworth	D-3

CHURCHES

9	Catedral Metropolitana	C-3
10	Del Corazón de Jesús	C-1
11	De La Concepción	B-1
12	Domingo Savio	A-1
13	La Asunción	B-2
14	La Merced	D-3
15	La Victoria	C-3
16	San Agustín	C-4
17	San Francisco	D-3
18	Santo Domingo	D-4

ART GALLERIES

19	Del Puerto	C-3
20	La Manzana Verde	A-6
21	Manging Art Gallery	A-5
22	Taller Guayasamín	A-6

CULTURAL CENTERS AND UNIVERSITIES*

23	Alianza Francesa	B-4
24	Politécnica del Litoral	D-4
25	Universidad Católica	A-4
26	Universidad de Guayaquil	B-4
27	Univ. Vicente Rocafuerte	C-5

* All these centers have important libraries

SHOPPING CENTERS

28	Las Vitrinas	B-5
29	Plaza Triángulo	A-5
30	Policentro	B-6
31	Unicentro	C-3

PRINCIPAL MARKETS

32	Artesanal	D-4
33	Central	C-3
34	De Flores	C-4
35	José Mascote	B-3
36	Municipal norte	D-4
37	Municipal oeste	B-3
38	Municipal sur	C-2
39	Santa Rosa	B-3

PARKS

40	Bolívar	C-3
41	Centenario	C-3
42	Urdesa	A-5
43	El Bosque	B-5
44	España	C-1
45	Guayaquil	B-4
46	La Concordia	C-5
47	Victoria	C-3

OTHERS

48	Airport	C-7
49	Las Peñas Neighborhood	D-4
50	Centro Cívico	B-1
51	Hemiciclo o Rotonda	D-3
4	Tower of El Reloj	D-3
4	Palacio Municipal	D-3

Legend

Hotel (luxury)
Hospital
Educational center
Sports center
Avenue
District name: LAS PEÑAS
Parks and recreational areas
Other green areas
Urban area
River / swamp

Cuenca and the Southern Highlands

CUENCA AND THE SOUTHERN HIGHLANDS

The southern highlands of Ecuador, known as the *Sierra Sur*, are geologically different from those in the north. They are the product of an older period of volcanic activity and have therefore been subject to erosion for a much longer time. As a result, the towering active snow-capped volcanoes of the north are replaced by lower gently rolling hills and broad rounded valleys in the south. This region is also less seismically active and enjoys a slightly milder climate.

The southern highlands are divided into three provinces, from north to south: **Cañar** (capital: Azogues), **Azuay** (Cuenca) and **Loja** (Loja).

THE CITY OF CUENCA

LOCATION AND GEOGRAPHY

The city of Cuenca is situated at 2.550 m. (8.364 ft.) above sea level in a broad inter-andean basin ringed by mountains. The city is crossed by two rivers, the Yanuncay and the Tomebamba. These join and flow eastwards to drain into the River Paute, which in turn descends the eastern slopes of the *cordillera* to the Amazon Basin.

The hills surrounding Cuenca are an excellent example of the inter-relationship between altitude, climate, vegetation and agriculture in the Andes. On the cold windswept tops, tussock grass and alpine tundra predominate. As one descends, one encounters the typical terraced andean agriculture, with subsistence crops best suited to each level appearing in roughly the following order, from top to bottom: potatoes, barley, peas, corn, beans and pasture. Lower still, toward the valley floors, one finds a wide variety of vegetables, fruit orchards and flowers alongside lush pasture land.

The climate of the city itself is quite similar to that of other intermont basins, with warm days, cool nights, and a mean temperature of 14° C (57° F). Nights can be particularly chilly during the southern hemisphere's winter, June through September. Annual precipitation seldom exceeds 800 mm. (31.5 in.).

HISTORY AND DEVELOPMENT

The region of Cuenca was inhabited in pre-columbian times by several indigenous tribes of considerable distinction, noted for their advanced civilizations. Due to its geographical location, it was among the earlier regions of what is now Ecuador to come under the influence of the Incas, as their empire expanded from south to north.

Some 70 km. (44 mi.) to the north of Cuenca, in an area known as *Hatun Cañar*, the Incas built the ceremonial center of *Ingapirca* which remains today as the most important Inca archeological site in all of Ecuador.

After the Spanish conquest, Cuenca became an important and populous regional center in the crown colony which was governed from Quito. Of particular interest to the *conquistadores* and the Spanish settlers who followed them, was the working of precious metals for which Cuenca's indigenous inhabitants had developed a well deserved reputation.
After independence from Spain, Cuenca was capital of one of the three provinces that made up the new republic, along with Quito and Guayaquil. Over the years it developed a reputation as a center of art and culture, being home to several well known poets, and even earned the nickname of "The Athens of Ecuador".

Today, Cuenca is Ecuador's third city and the commercial, industrial and transportation center of the three provinces that make up the southern highlands. The city has enjoyed considerable economic growth in recent years but has not lost its colonial charm or its tranquil atmosphere.
The native people of Cuenca and its environs, particularly the women who are refered to as *Cholas Cuencanas*, have maintained their own distinctive dress and adornments. The Spanish spoken in and around Cuenca has a unique lilting intonation.

CHURCHES

The Old Cathedral:
Address: Luis Cordero corner Mariscal Sucre.
This was the original *El Sagrario* church built at the time of the founding of the city. It included Inca stone benches taken from the Inca's *Pumapungo* Palace. It has been restored and today houses a fine concert hall with am impressive organ.

The New Cathedral:
Address: Benigno Malo and Mariscal Sucre.
Phone: 842-097
A magnificent blue domed structure with a marble interior and massive gold altar. It is one of the most impressive churches in Ecuador and one of the largest in all of Latin America.

La Concepción:
Address: Hermano Miguel 633, between Pres. Córdova and Juan Jaramillo.
Phone: 823-002
The adjoining monastery's museum has an good display of religious and popular art.

San Blas:
Address: Manuel Vega between Simón Bolívar and Mariscal Sucre.
Phone: 822-899
Built in 1575 with stones taken from the *Pumapungo* Palace.

San Francisco:
Address: Córdova between General Torres and Padre Aguirre.
Phone: 822-987
Its interior has baroque decorations and the pulpit is particularly impressive.

Convento Santo Domingo:
Address: Gran Colombia between General Torres and Padre Aguirre.
Phone: 827-115
This church with its double towers dates back to the early days of the colonial period.

MUSEUMS

Archeological Museum of the Central Bank:
Address: Larga corner Huayna-Cápac.
Phone: 831-255
Located by the ruins of the *Pumapungo* Palace. This was once the palace of *Atahualpa*, the last Inca ruler. It was partly destroyed during the Inca civil war.
Following the Spanish conquest many of the stones were taken to build Cuenca's main churches and other colonial structures. The museum houses artifacts from excavation of the pre-columbian settlement of *Tomebamba*.

Hours: Monday to Friday: 9:00 - 18:00 hrs.
Saturday: 9:00 - 13:00 hrs.

Casa de la Cultura:
Address: Luis Cordero corner Sucre, 2nd fl.
Phone: 836-935
Art gallery and museum.

Hours: Monday to Friday: 9:00-13:00 & 15:00-18:00 hrs.

Museum of Modern Art:
Address: Plaza San Sebastián, Sucre and Talbot.
Phone: 831-027
Housed in a lovely colonial building, this municipal museum is known for its contemporary paintings.
It is the home of the *"Bienal de Pintura"* international painting exhibition.

Hours: Monday to Friday: 9:00-13:00 & 15:00-19:00 hrs.
Saturday & Sunday: 10:00 - 13:00 hrs.

Instituto Azuayo de Folklore:
Address: Cordero 722 and Sucre, third floor.
Phone: 830-016
Houses a fine collection of folk art.

Hours: Monday to Friday: 8:30-12:00 & 14:30-18:00 hrs.

SHOPPING

Cuenca is famous for its ceramics, gold and silver jewelry, as well as a variety of leather goods, textiles and other crafts. *Sombreros de paja toquilla* (Panama hats) are worn and sold in this part of the country, although many are in fact produced in the province of Manabí, on the Pacific coast. Many craft shops are concentrated along Benigno Malo and also along Gran Colombia.

PLACES OF INTEREST NEAR CUENCA

Ingapirca: Ecuador's best known Inca ruins are described below under the province of Cañar in which they are located.

The Paute River Valley: Located some 25 km. (15,5 mi.) east of Cuenca, this is the traditional weekend and holiday playground of the city's residents. It has a somewhat lower altitude and consequently a slightly warmer climate than Cuenca itself. Most of the valley is given over to agriculture, with lush pasture land and fruit orchards worked by the area's industrious residents. The atmosphere is most pleasant and relaxing.

The following are some of the better known towns in the valley. **Gualaceo** has a lovely location and several excellent resort hotels nearby. **Chordeleg** is famous for its jewelers and goldsmiths as well as the colorful *Paso del Niño* (Procession of the "Christ" Child) which takes place on New Year's Eve. **Paute** also has a pleasant location and is known for its alcoholic beverages which are distilled from the locally grown sugar cane.

Cajas: This is a 28.808 Hectares (71.186 Acres) National Recreation Area situated 35 km. (22 mi.) northwest of Cuenca. It features rare high altitude flora and fauna, including condors, and a chain of 232 small lakes; some at over 4.000 m. (13.000 ft.) altitude. There is trout fishing and the views are breathtaking, but the climate is cold and damp. Visitors should take adequate clothing, and for those staying overnight, shelter and provisions.

PROVINCES OF THE SOUTHERN HIGHLANDS

CAÑAR

This province is located north of Cuenca and has its capital in the city of **Azogues**.

Ingapirca: Ecuador's best known Inca ruins are located 36 km. (22 mi.) north of Azogues near the town of **Cañar**. The area of *Ingapirca* was inhabited by the *Cañari* indians in pre-Inca times. In the 15th century the region was conquered by the Inca *Tupac Yupanqui* and his warriors. Over time the *Cañaris* came to be one of the Inca's most faithful allies. The Inca *Huayna-Cápac* was born in this area and it was he who decreed the construction of the great ceremonial center whose name signifies "the wall of the Inca".
Ingapirca was both a center of ritual ceremonies and a meeting place for the population as a whole. The central structure of the complex, a large elliptical platform hewn out of a hillside, may well have served as a solar observatory. The sun *(Inti)* was the Inca's principal deity and it was to it that they offered their sacrifices. In addition, it may have been from this high platform that the Inca, surrounded by his court and nobility, addressed his subjects gathered below.
There is a small but excellent museum on the site, administered by the Central Bank (hours: Tuesday to Saturday: 9:00 - 17:00 hrs.). It displays artifacts from both the *Cañari* and Inca periods along with detailed explanations of their significance. The displays are in Spanish but guidebooks and guides speaking other languages are generally available.

AZUAY

This province has **Cuenca** as its capital and was described in the preceding section.

LOJA

This is the southernmost province of the Ecuadorian highlands, and its capital bears the same name. The town of **Saraguro**, situated 62 km. (38,5 mi.) north of the capital along the road to Cuenca, is well known for its colorful Sunday market. The native inhabitants of the area have a very distinctive form of dress. The men wear black short trousers and broad brimmed hats. The women use pleated black skirts, colorful bead necklaces, and a unique silver ornamental pin, the Topo, in their shawls.

Vilcabamba: Located 62 km. (38,5 mi.) south of the city of Loja in a broad fertile valley, this town had developed a reputation as a fountain of youth with many of its inhabitants supposedly living well beyond 100 years.

Despite extensive scientific investigation, much controversy remains as to the possible reasons for this phenomenon, and its very authenticity has been called into question. None-the-less, there are many people in their eighties, nineties and beyond living in this region whereas Ecuadorians as a whole have a life expectancy of 66 years. Whatever the case may be, the area has nice scenery, a pleasant mild climate, and is most definitely peaceful and relaxing.

The Amazon Basin

THE AMAZON BASIN

LOCATION AND GEOGRAPHY

East of the Andes lies Ecuador's tropical jungle known as *El Oriente.* It is a humid, hilly basin, drained by large rivers, which flood vast expanses of land and eventually flow to the Amazon. The low *Cordillera Oriental*, Ecuador's easternmost range of the Andes lies on the western edge of this basin. The flanks of these andean foothills, are covered in rain and cloud forests, which thrive in this persistently humid environment. The scenery in this region is very beautiful.

The Ecuadorian Amazon is divided into five provinces. These are the country's largest and the least densely populated. They are, from north to south: **Sucumbíos** (capital: Nueva Loja, more commonly known as Lago Agrio), **Napo** (Tena), **Pastaza** (Puyo), **Morona Santiago** (Macas) and **Zamora Chinchipe** (Zamora).

RUSHING TORRENTS AND MEANDERING RIVERS

The constant precipitation has molded the geography to create a complex drainage system. Rushing torrents of white water abound in the foothills of the Andes. As these reach the jungle, they turn into wide meandering rivers, tributaries of the mighty Amazon. These rivers carry much sediment and therefore have a muddy, *café au lait*, appearance. The broad channel, turbid color, and winding course of these jungle rivers combine to give the false impression that they are slow moving, when in fact the current is often perilously swift. An immense variety of fish and other species are found in these waters.

Caution is advised for those who might want to swim. The fast flow can easily drag a person downstream, there is the risk of acquiring skin infections, and of course the odd *piraña*. Inquire with the locals before diving in.

Long dugout canoes, with powerful outboard motors, are commonly used on the jungle rivers for passenger and merchandise transport. Navigation is best left to those familiar with a particular river, due to the presence of numerous sandbanks, strong currents, and unpredictable eddies.

THE PRIMEVAL RAINFOREST

Due to the intense humidity and heat, vegetation is abundant and its growth rate is very high. Many species of plants, ranging from low grass to large trees that grow to over 30 m. (100 ft.) in height, create both a thick ground cover and a dense high canopy.
Each plant and animal species has adapted to survive as part of the tropical forest, finding its own niche in this complex ecosystem. For example, some giant trees have de-

veloped external roots, in addition to their main root system. These roots act as guys which help to support their towering trunks. Smaller plants have exceptionally wide leaves, of various shapes, adapted to capture as much as possible of the scarce sunlight which manages to filter through the upper canopy.

The visitor is struck by the exuberance of life in the jungle; by its ostentatiousness in size, color, and diversity. One is easily mesmerized by the sight of giant Blue Morpho butterflies flittering in a ray of sunshine, the sweet perfume of flowers borne on the breeze, the sound of a troop of monkeys swinging through the treetops, or a fleeting glimpse of giant macaws on the wing.

It is worth remembering however, that the competition for survival is particularly intense in this environment and that other species adaptations represent special hazards for the visitor. Some species of trees bear long and extremely sharp spines on their trunks, others are protected by colonies of stinging ants, and still others like well known *curaray* (cuarare) contain deadly poisons. Venomous snakes and giant constrictors, the *anacondas*, are to be found throughout the region as are a wide variety of stinging insects, some of which are vectors of serious diseases such as Malaria and Yellow Fever.

The turnover of life is extremely rapid in the jungle. Everything seems to bloom in a great hurry, and decay in equally short order. There is constant vague aroma of fermentation hanging in the heavy air.

The area has long been a source of both fear and fascination to outsiders. The explorer Francisco de Orellana traveled from Quito to the mouth of the Amazon in 1542 and is credited with being the first European to make the journey. His journal speaks of an almost magical land of cloves and cinnamon, of warrior women for whom he named the world's largest river, and of seven months of navigation through the heart of the unknown. More sobering is the fact that his expedition left Quito with a party of almost 5000 men, and arrived at the Atlantic with only 80. Orellana mounted a second expedition in 1546, and never again emerged from the jungle.

Today's visitor to the Ecuadorian Amazon can enjoy the satisfaction of discovery with considerably fewer risks. None-the-less, prudence is advised. Malaria prophylaxis and vaccination against Yellow Fever are important, as are travel with experienced guides or appropriate groups. Independent travel is by no means ruled out for those who know what they are doing, but this is definitely not a place for the inexperienced to wander off on their own. No less than the high mountains or the open sea, the jungle demands the respect of all who would experience its wonders in safety.

MAN AND HIS ECONOMIC ACTIVITIES IN THE JUNGLE

Natural Resources: In an attempt to survive and in the name of "progress", man has traveled to and invaded all geographical regions of our planet. Tropical jungles were traditionally feared and avoided by outsiders. However, with a rapid increase in population and a greater demand for agricultural land, man was forced to widen his horizons. Trails and roads were cut into the jungle and with this the deforestation began. The use of wood for construction in the cities as well as the country has led to a great decrease in the number of woodlands. The tropical forests of the world are quickly disappearing.

In Ecuador, two million Hectares (5 million Acres) of Amazon jungle have been cleared in the last 20 years, in order to plant crops and create pastures. Man's greatest incursion in the Ecuadorian jungle has taken place since the 1970's due to petroleum exploration. There are more than 300 oil wells, hundreds of kilometers of pipelines, refineries and other installations which have direct or indirect impact on the jungle's fragile environment.

Tourism: A number of travel companies offer organized group tours to locations of particular natural beauty or scientific interest in the *Oriente*. There are also many licensed guides who provide private tours and independent travel to the region is likewise possible. There are commercial flights from Quito to Nueva Loja (Lago Agrio), Puerto Francisco Orellana (Coca), and Macas. The national oil company flies to Tarapoa and the army to Shell and Gualaquiza. There is also bus service throughout the area. Road access from the highlands is possible via four routes from: Quito, Ambato, Cuenca and Loja. Road surfaces are generally gravel or graded earth and a 4-wheel-drive vehicle is recommended for those who wish to drive. The principal means of public transport within the more remote regions of the *Oriente* is by river. The canoes used for this service can also be hired for touring.

The Napo River is one of the most frequently visited areas, from the port of Misahuallí (access through Tena), down river as far as Limoncocha. Puerto Francisco Orellana (Coca) is another important access point to this river. Other places of interest are Shushufindi, an agricultural cooperative in the northernmost province of Sucumbíos, Nueva Loja (Lago Agrio) capital of the same province, Macas and Sucúa in the province of Morona Santiago and Zamora, capital of Zamora Chinchipe in the south.
One interesting trip by land, in the northern *Oriente* takes you through Baeza, along the *Quijos* River, by the active Reventador Volcano, past the San Rafael Falls and on to Nueva Loja (Lago Agrio). From there, you can continue deeper into the jungle, following the roads opened for oil exploration, one of which leads you to the Cuyabeno Fauna Reserve (see national parks section). Along the way,

agricultural settlements, beautiful rivers such as the Aguarico and Eno, primary forests and small lakes such as the Laguna de Lago Agrio, can be admired. Those with sufficient time available to them can make the return trip going south from Nueva Loja (Lago Agrio) to Puerto Francisco Orellana (Coca) and on to Sarayacu. Returning to the highlands either via Baeza or Tena.

THE PEOPLE OF THE AMAZON

Today, the character of the population of *Oriente* is mixed. With the opening of several access roads, people of other regions of the country moved to the jungle in search of a better life. Many cattle ranches and agricultural settlements are found throughout the region. Towns have developed because of the oil exploration, which has attracted many people to the area. Others have moved to this region to prospect for gold.

All the migration to the *Oriente*, as well as missionary activity and tourism have encroached on the lives of the native people who have inhabited this region for thousands of years. Their customs and traditions, very well suited for survival in the jungle have been altered with the arrival of the outsiders.

The awareness of the need to preserve the cultural heritage of the native people of the Ecuadorian Amazon has increased in recent years. In 1980, the Confederation of Indigenous Nations of the Ecuadorian Amazon (COFENIAE) was created. This entity is in charge of organizing the different cultural groups, defending their land rights, and creating agricultural, educational and health programs, suited to the needs of this population.

The following are the main indigenous tribes or nations which live in the Ecuadorian Amazon. The **Quichuas** are a broad linguistic group numbering about 60,000 people who live near the foothills of the Andes. Their language is likely the result of influence from their highland neighbors. The Quichuas from the Napo river region are known as the **Quijos**. The **Jívaros** or **Shuar** also speak *Quichua* and are best known for their now abandoned practice of head hunting and shrinking. The **Cofanes**, who live along the border with Colombia, have only 600 members in Ecuador and are clearly in danger of extinction. The **Sionas** and **Secoyas**, a group of only 500, live in the Cuyabeno-Shushufindi area of the province of Sucumbíos. Finally the **Huaoranis** or **Aucas**, numbering about 1700, live in the Yasuní area of Napo Province.

Due to the recent colonization of the Amazon, the native people have lost much of their land and have been forced to relocate and change their lifestyle. Those living near the modern towns participate in the local economy, growing crops or raising animals for sale. Those living in the remaining remote areas carry on with more traditional activities such as hunting, fishing, gathering and subsistence farming. The latter takes place in small plots, which are cleared in the jungle, without cutting the larger trees. These are farmed for a few years and then abandoned, allowing the soil and jungle vegetation to recover. Naturally, the outside world has introduced changes to even the most isolated areas. For example, the shotgun is today more popular than the blowgun and spear, although these too continue to be used.

Although some of the traditions have been lost and not every native paints his body or wears feathers, a strong cultural identity remains. These people's world vision, with man as an integral part of the jungle, remains unchanged. Customary beliefs still hold, traditional medicine is practiced and witch-doctors continue to play an important, albeit diminished, role in society.

Protected Areas

PROTECTED AREAS

Ecuador is a small and very densely populated country in which most of the land has been taken up by agriculture and habitation. In an effort to preserve those natural areas of particular scenic or scientific interest, 15 areas were set aside as national parks or nature reserves in the 1970s. These parks are administered by the Forestry and Renewable Natural Resources Department of the Ministry of Agriculture. There is an entrance fee for visitors to those parks which have an organized infrastructure.

GALAPAGOS NATIONAL PARK

This is Ecuador's best known National Park and was included in the UNESCO's World Heritage Trust in 1979. The Galápagos Archipelago is also one of Ecuador's 21 provinces and has its capital in **Puerto Baquerizo Moreno** on the island of San Cristóbal.

HISTORY

Tomás de Berlanga discovered these uninhabited islands in 1535. During the following centuries the archipelago became the safe haven of pirates and buccaneers. They did much damage by introducing previously absent land mammals to the islands and depleting the giant turtle population. These reptiles were considered an ideal source of food as they could be stored alive onboard ship for extended periods of time. In 1830, Ecuador annexed the islands, with the initial intention of turning them into agricultural settlements. When this failed, they became a penal colony and remained so until 1958.
The Galápagos Archipelago is of great interest to scientists from around the world, who visit the islands to study this unique habitat and its plant and animal species. Probably the best known visitor to the islands was Charles Darwin, who spent several months studying them in 1835 as naturalist onboard *The Beagle*, during its five year voyage around the world. His observations on the Galápagos and data he obtained there, were of utmost importance in his formulation of the theory of evolution through natural selection. In honor of Darwin and to commemorate the 100th anniversary of the publication of *The Origin of the Species*, the Charles Darwin Research Institute was created in 1959. This institute is located on Santa Cruz Island. It is in charge of research regarding the endemic species of the islands and plays an important role in the administration of the National Park.

LOCATION AND GEOGRAPHY

The Galápagos Archipelago is located 900 to 1.000 km. (560 to 620 mi.) west of the Ecuadorian coastline. It lies along the equator, between 89° 16' and 92° 11' west longitude and between 1° 50' north and 1° 50' south latitude.

The islands are of volcanic origin and sit at the junction of the Nazca and Cocos tectonic plates. They cover a surface area of approximately 8.000 km.^{2} (3.088 mi.^{2}). Over half of this surface area, 4.710 km.^{2} (1.918 mi.^{2}) corresponds to Isabela, the largest island. There are 8 main islands, 6 smaller islands and many islets spread over a large expanse of ocean. Some of the smaller islands are bordered by huge cliffs and cannot by accessed from the sea. The accumulation of coral and sea shells the beaches of others, gives the shorelines a special luminosity which stands out from the surrounding turquoise green ocean set against the dark background of volcanic rocks. The volcanic activity which gave rise to the Galápagos started approximately 3 million years ago. Since that time, the archipelago has been formed and molded into a truly unique geography. Evidence of current volcanic activity can be seen on the islands of Isabela and Fernandina, both of which have volcanoes which are still smoking. As one sails from east to west, one encounters progressively newer islands.

Many volcanic cones of different shapes are found in the islands. The volcanic activity is characterized by constant stream of molten lava gradually gliding down to the sea, rather than by sudden violent eruptions. The highest of the many peaks on the islands is *Cerro Azul*, on Isabela. It reaches 1.689 m. (5.440 ft.) above sea level but the absolute height of this mountain, when measured from the ocean floor, is some 4.500 m. (14.800 ft.). Some of the islands however, were created by the tectonic uplifting of underwater basalt platforms and are therefore perfectly flat.

When molten lava reaches the ocean and cools suddenly, it solidifies into the most unusual shapes. The pattern created by the flow of lava is particularly noticeable at Sullivan Bay on Santiago Island. A flow from only 100 years ago covers an area of approximately 100 km.^{2} (38,6 mi.^{2}). The new lava is still very distinct from the older rock which has started to decay. The surface has ripples which show clearly it once was a liquid flowing towards the sea.
Near the Island of Floreana, there is a sunken crater, with peaks along its circular rim, sticking out of the ocean. It has been dubbed *La Corona del Diablo* (The Devil's Crown).

CLIMATE

The climate of Galápagos is influenced by its geographical location along the equator, the cold Humboldt ocean current flowing up from Antarctica, the annual *El Niño* climatic phenomenon and the mountains of the larger islands which trap moisture from the prevailing ocean winds. From June to December, strong southeasterly winds prevail, temperatures range between 18° and 20°C (64° to 68°F), and there is some fog and mist. In September and October, there can be torrential rains. Between January and May, the wind diminishes, and the temperatures rise to between 24° and 28°C (75° to 82°F).

The islands are very dry. Although they can sometimes receive heavy rains, this water is quickly washed out to sea because of the hard, impermeable basalt. Water only accumulates in the craters and rock cracks. This inability to conserve rain water and the equatorial heat, have rendered what soil the islands have very arid.

VEGETATION

Due to the rocky nature of the islands, only spiny and very spindly vegetation grows in the lower altitudes. On recent lava flows, there is no vegetation at all. As cracks form in the lava and bits of soil gets trapped in them, pioneer species can take root. The few trees that grow below 200 m. (656 ft.), have only few, small leaves. On the foothills there are *algarrobos* (carob trees) and bushes known as *palo santo*. The larger dry plains have giant cacti which grow to several meters in height. The trunks and branches of these cacti constitute important sweet water reservoirs in this very arid environment. There are also some lichens which trap the humidity in the air, in order to grow.

Above 200 m. (656 ft.), temperatures are cooler, there is more humidity and the vegetation becomes thicker and greener. There is a grassy ground cover, the tree trunks are thicker and the foliage more abundant. There are many *guayaba (guava)* trees and citrus trees, both introduced from the continent. All the islands have their own endemic plants as well as those common to several islands which were generally introduced by man.

FAUNA

The Galápagos' unique fauna is renowned for its diversity and because the islands constitute a natural laboratory, in which the evolution of the species through natural selection can be studied. A prime example is that of the finches, studied in detail by Darwin. Each variety of this small bird has developed its own unique traits, according to the needs imposed by the particular habitat in which it must survive. Each island has its own endemic species and many of these are not found anywhere else in the world. The reptile, bird and marine life of the islands is extremely rich.

Among the reptiles, the giant galápagos tortoise, which has given the islands their name, is the best known. These can be seen traveling in groups towards their watering holes, or stretching their long necks to feed from the giant cacti. Some can live up to 300 years. They are most common in the highlands of Isabela and smaller numbers exist in six other islands. The seaweed eating, marine iguanas are the only sea-going lizard in the world. They can be seen on most of the islands although because of their black color, they camouflage very well on the basalt rocks of shores. The larger land iguanas are also well adapted to camouflage with the dry surroundings. There are also a number of smaller species of lizards and non-venomous snakes, but no frogs or toads. The land and marine bird life is also exceptionally varied.

There are among others: Galápagos hawks; Darwin's finches (mentioned previously); mockingbirds; Galápagos waved albatross, which nest on Española; masked, blue footed, and red footed boobies; frigate birds; flamingos; dusky lava gulls; Galápagos doves; red-billed tropic birds; and Galápagos penguins.
Among the mammals are the Galápagos sea lions which can be found by many islands and the less common Galápagos fur-seals, by the rockier shores. Dolphins abound in the waters surrounding the entire archipelago. All the land mammals found on the islands have been introduced by man. Horses, donkeys, goats, pigs, dogs, cats, rats and mice are all found wild in many locations. There is a campaign to exterminate these foreign species, which pose a grave danger to the native fauna and flora.
The marine life is also very rich. One quarter of the species of fish found in the Galápagos waters are unique to this area. There are also crabs, lobsters and many other crustaceans.

ACCESS

There are daily flights from Quito and Guayaquil to Baltra for Puerto Ayora (Santa Cruz Island) and three flights a week to Puerto Baquerizo Moreno (San Cristóbal Island). Although accommodations are available in both these locations, and camping is permitted in few designated areas, by far the best way to experience the islands is by sailing amongst them. A wide variety of vessels, ranging from the spartan to the opulent, are available for this purpose. Most visitors book tours and cruises on the mainland, but last minute arrangements are sometimes possible on site.

COTOPAXI NATIONAL PARK

This park is located 53 km. (32 mi.) south of Quito and includes the *Cotopaxi* and *Rumiñahui* volcanoes and the surrounding areas in the provinces of Cotopaxi, Pichincha and Napo. Cotopaxi is a beautiful snow capped volcano, standing 5.850 m. (19.342 ft.) above sea level, on the central *Cordillera* of the Andes. It is the world's highest active volcano and some of its most devastating eruptions took place only 200 years ago. Evidence of the volcanic activity can be seen everywhere: enormous boulders, solidified lava, ash, and huge mud slides that were caused when the mountain's massive glaciers were suddenly melted by fiery lava. Cotopaxi is a world-class mountaineering challenge but you don't have to a climber to visit this volcano, and the view on a clear day is most rewarding.
From the park's entry station, just off the Panamerican Highway, a good gravel road leads 35 km. (22 mi.) through pine forest and then over a high plateau to a parking area at the base of a large field of volcanic ash at 4.600 m. (14.988 ft.). From here it is a one hour stiff walk to the climbers' shelter at the snow line. The shelter is open to climbers and day visitors alike and is equipped with bunk beds and cooking facilities.

Rumiñahui (Stone Face) is also impressive, a dormant volcano with a particularly craggy appearance. Between it and Cotopaxi lies the high plateau of *Limpio-Pungo* and the lake of the same name. The area has rare high altitude flora and small groups of wild horses can sometimes be seen here.

MACHALILLA NATIONAL PARK

This coastal park is located in the province of Manabí. It encompasses 3.500 Hectares (8.650 Acres), including the offshore islands of *La Plata* and *Salango*. The park has some spectacular scenery: magnificent beaches, bays, cliffs, islands and islets, all in their natural state.
The park contains the last remaining dry tropical forest in Ecuador, in addition to corral reefs in the area surrounding Isla de La Plata. It also has archeological potential as remains from the *Manteño* culture have been found in the park, near the village of Agua Blanca.
At this time, the park does not have much in the way of infrastructure for visitors, however, its scenic beauty can be admired from the Salango - Puerto López - Machalilla - Puerto Cayo road. *Los Piqueros* (the boobies) lookout is just minutes south of Puerto López, it offers some excellent photographic possibilities.
The Agua Blanca archeological site can be reached by car, 5 km. (3 mi.) east off the Puerto López-Machalilla Road. There is an exhibit in Puerto López, showing the park's natural resources, flora and fauna. The archeology museum, in the town of Salango, has a small but excellent exhibit about the ancient coastal cultures of Ecuador.

PODOCARPUS NATIONAL PARK

This park is located in the southeast of Ecuador, straddling the provinces of Loja and Zamora Chinchipe. It features a very lush cloud forest with abundant flora and fauna. The huge clouds that boil up form the Amazon basin are blown west by the prevailing winds. When these are forced upwards into colder air by the Andes, they condense, turning into rain and mist. The cloud forests, also known as *ceja andina* (the eyebrow of the Andes) thrive in this environment. A large variety of epiphytes; orchids, mosses, lichens and bromeliads are all to be found in Podocarpus. The park is also home to the endangered spectacled bear and numerous species of birds.
One access road to Podocarpus begins approximately 15 km. (9 mi.) south of Loja, off the Loja-Vilcabamba road. It is about 6 km. (4 mi.) from the turnoff to the park gate. There are also two accesses on the Zamora side of the park. Permits must be obtained from the Ministry of Agriculture in Loja or Zamora. The Park's Headquarters and a refuge are 1 km. (0,6 mi.) from the Zamora entrance. Camping is possible in the park but no supplies are available locally, and it is advisable to bring supplies from the larger towns.

SANGAY NATIONAL PARK

This park was included in UNESCO's World Heritage Trust in 1984. It is located in the area where the provinces of Chimborazo, Morona Santiago and Tungurahua meet. The park encompasses a great variety of geographical regions. There are three important volcanoes within the park: *Tungurahua*, *El Altar* and *Sangay*. The latter is active and eruptions take place at intervals of 10 to 25 minutes. The park has a great diversity of scenery, flora and fauna. The glaciers of El Altar at 5.319 m. (17.446 ft.) above sea level give way to high *páramos* (moorlands), and these in turn yield to the cloud forests of the eastern slopes of the Andes descending to their subtropical foothills, at the edge of the Amazon basin. Like Podocarpus, Sangay National Park is home to the spectacled bear. The bird life in the park ranges from the condor of the higher altitudes to the macaws and toucans of the subtropical forests. The park's flora is unusual, because of the climatic influence from the dry southern lowlands.
Access to the northern end of the park is from the village of Pondoa, approximately 10 km. (6 mi.) southwest of Baños. There is a shelter for mountaineers on Tungurahua at 3.800 m. (12.464 ft.), 4 to 6 hours hike up from Pondoa. From the shelter to the snow line is about 3 to 4 hours and it takes approximately 1 hour from there to the summit. Crampons, ice axes, and some experience are required. Another access point to the park is past Candelaria, a small village reached from the town of Penipe in the province of Chimborazo. The trail going from this access goes to the eroded crater of El Altar. The hike to the crater, where you can camp, takes approximately 9 hours. The scenery is magnificent. The climb to the summits of El Altar is extremely difficult and only for very experienced climbers. There is a road between Pungalá (Chimborazo) and Huamboya (Morona Santiago) which goes right through the park. It passes between El Altar and Sangay.
A different area of the park can be accessed from the southeast, between the town of Macas and the village of 9 de Octubre or, alternatively, between Macas and the mission of Sevilla-Don Bosco. The climb to Sangay is also for very experienced mountaineers and requires two days. One has to be quite lucky to catch a glimpse of Sangay, as it is usually shrouded in mist. If one is fortunate, the sight of smoke coming out of the snow covered cone is breathtaking.
There is a National Park office in Riobamba, at the corner of Primera Constituyente and Pichincha.

YASUNI NATIONAL PARK

This park is located in the Napo River basin, in the province of the same name. Yasuní's forest is special because of its age. It is one of the rain forest islands which survived the last ice age, and is therefore much older than the most of the forests in the Amazon basin.

The park is the home of the *Huaorani* nation. It is also very rich in flora and fauna. This is the habitat of innumerable species of insects, reptiles, marsupials and mammals.
The main access to the park is from the north, via the Napo River.

CAJAS NATIONAL PARK

See **Cajas** under "Places of Interest near Cuenca".

Other National Parks:

- Sumaco - Napo Galeras

COTACACHI - CAYAPAS ECOLOGICAL RESERVE

This reserve is located in the northwest of Ecuador in the provinces of Imbabura and Esmeraldas. It spans the Western *Cordillera* of the Andes and the northern Pacific lowlands. In the highlands it includes the Cotacachi volcano (4.939 m.; 16.200 ft.) and Lake Cuicocha (see Imbabura in the northern highlands section). In the lowlands it covers a very lush, primary, tropical forest.
The reserve is home to the *Chachis* nation, commonly known as the *Cayapas*, because they live on the shores of the Cayapas River. These people lead a traditional life. The *La Tolita* Cultural Monument, an archeological site is also part of the Cotacachi-Cayapas Reserve.
Access to the reserve is through Cuicocha (described earlier) and by river from the town of Borbón in Esmeraldas. The National Park Service offers tours of up to 5 days in the lowland area of the reserve.

CAYAMBE - COCA ECOLOGICAL RESERVE

This reserve is located in the area where the provinces of Pichincha, Imbabura, Sucumbíos and Napo meet. It includes the *Cayambe* and *Reventador* volcanoes.
Reaching 5.790 m. (18.991 ft.), Cayambe is the highest point on earth along the equator and the only place in the world where both the latitude and temperature reach zero degrees simultaneously. The climb to the summit is technical and quite dangerous, as there are many crevasses. There is a shelter for climbers. It is accessed via a 26 km. (16 mi.) cobbled road, starting just south of the town of Cayambe. From the road it is approximately 4 hours hike to the shelter. Reventador, the second volcano found within the reserve, is still active. It is located on the eastern range of the Andes, the *Cordillera Oriental*.

MANGLARES - CHURUTE ECOLOGICAL RESERVE

This reserve is located in the province of Guayas, on the shores of the Gulf of Guayaquil, southeast of the delta of the Guayas River. Several small rivers flow out to sea through the reserve, creating islands which are fringed by mangroves. The reserve is rich in bird and aquatic life. To access to the reserve from the north, turn south 21 km. (13 mi.) east of Guayaquil, on the Guayaquil-El Triunfo road. From the east, turn west off the El Triunfo-Naranjal road, 21 km. (13 mi.) north of Naranjal.

Other Ecological Reserves:

- Antisana
- El Angel
- Los Ilinizas
- Mache Chindul

LIMONCOCHA BIOLOGICAL RESERVE

This wildlife reserve is located on the north shore of the Napo River, approximately 45 km. (28 mi.) down river from Puerto Francisco Orellana (Coca). It includes an ancient lake which is very rich in aquatic life, some of which is unique. The area is most scenic and there is abundant wildlife. Access to the reserve is via the Napo River. Accommodations can be arranged.

CHIMBORAZO FAUNA RESERVE

This reserve is located on the northwestern slopes of Mount Chimborazo, in the province of Bolívar. It was created as part of a project aimed at reintroducing vicuñas to Ecuador. These graceful wild relatives of the llamas and alpacas had been extinct in Ecuador for some two centuries. In 1988, two groups of vicuñas were transported from northern Chile and southern Perú to the Chimborazo reserve, a habitat in which vicuñas had lived in the past. For the moment they are confined the reserve's boundaries, but when their numbers will be large enough, they will be allowed to roam free. Access to the reserve is via a rough gravel road heading east off the Ambato-Guaranda road approximately 35 km. (22 mi.) from Ambato. The turnoff is marked with a red sign.

CUYABENO FAUNA RESERVE

This reserve is located in the province of Sucumbíos, between the San Miguel and Aguarico rivers. It encompasses a region of tropical rainforest, rich in Amazonian flora and fauna. The reserve is home to the Siona Nation, a small group of people who lead a traditional life. There are several beautiful lakes within the reserve.

The National Park Service maintains two cabins for visitors' use. Entrance permits can be obtained in Nueva Loja (Lago Agrio), Tarapoa or at the junction of the Cuyabeno and Aguarico rivers.

Transport to the reserve is via river. One embarkation point is on the Aguas Negras (Tarapuy) River. This point is accessed from *La Y*, at km. 85 on the Nueva Loja - Tarapoa - Tipishca road. There is a 2 km. (1,2 mi.) walk from *La Y* to the bridge over the Aguas Negras River. The canoe trip from this point to the lakes where the cabins are located takes 3 to 5 hours, depending on the level of the river. A second route is by land from Nueva Loja to Chiritza, km. 50 on the Tarapoa-Tipishca road. From there by motorized canoe, down the Aguarico River to the junction with the Cuyabeno and up the Cuyabeno to the lakes takes approximately 10 to 12 hours. A third alternative is by river from Puerto Aguarico, just south of Nueva Loja. Down the Aguarico to the junction with the Cuyabeno, and up the Cuyabeno to the lakes; a 14 to 15 hour trip.

PULULAHUA GEO-BOTANICAL RESERVE

See **Pululahua** under "Places of Interest near Quito".

EL BOLICHE NATIONAL RECREATION AREA

The El Boliche National Recreation Area is located at the base of the Cotopaxi volcano, along the southwestern boundary of Cotopaxi National Park. The access road off the Panamerican Highway is marked with a large sign. El Boliche features pine and cypress forests, picnic and camping areas, rustic cabins for overnight stay, nature trails and lovely scenery. Llamas and two species of deer are being reintroduced into the area.

Protected Wild Life Area:

- Pasochoa

HOTELS

PROVINCE: ESMERALDAS

CITY	CATEG.	ADDRESS	PHONE
ESMERALDAS			**(06)**
Hoteles:			
Esmeraldas	1st.	Av. Libertad 407	728703
Estuario Internacional	2nd.	Av. Libertad y G.Colombia	721300
Del Mar	2nd.	Av. Kennedy y Palmas	723707
Hostales:			
Cayapas	1st.	Av. Kennedy y Valdéz	721318
Ambato	2nd.	Av. Kennedy y Guerra	721144
El Galeón	2nd.	Piedrahita y Olmedo	723818
La Vega	2nd.	Olmedo y Rocafuerte	727014
Sultana de Los Andes	2nd.	Olmedo y 9 de Octubre	
Hostales Residencia:			
Americano	2nd.	Sucre y M. Cañizares	723768
Costa Esmeraldas	2nd.	Sucre y Piedrahita	710606
Sandry	2nd.	Av. Libertad y J. Montalvo	726861
Teisa	2nd.	Entrada a la Universidad	710030
Vasco	2nd.	Eloy Alfaro 523 y Mejía	710095
Hosterías:			
La Pradera	1st.	Km. 7.5 vía Atacames	712946
Marinos Inn	1st.	Av. Kennedy 1135	722227
Apartamentos Turísticos:			
Costa Verde	1st.	Luis Tello 809	728714
ATACAMES			
Hoteles:			
Casa Blanca	1st.	Barrio Nueva Granada	731031
Castelnuovo	1st.	Km. 25 vía Atacames	731046
Tiburón	2nd.	Malecón Playas	731145
Hostales:			
Nueva Granada	1st.	Barrio Nueva Granada	731399
Azucena	2nd.	Las Acacias	731139
Bachita	2nd.	Entrada a la Playa	731075
Delicias del Mar	2nd.	Entrada a la Playa	731076
Jennyfer	2nd.	Transversal la Playa	710482
Riandy Internacional	2nd.	Las Acacias	731247
Seaquarium	2nd.	Las Acacias	731091
Hostales Residencia:			
Atacames Inn	2nd.	Entrada a la Playa	731051
Chavalito	2nd.	Malecón del Río	731113
María Corina	2nd.	Entrada a la Playa	731302
Nuevo Hotel Atacames	2nd.	9 de Octubre	731020
Las Vegas	2nd.	Centro del pueblo	731039
Venecia	2nd.	Barrio Nueva Granada	731093
Hosterías:			
Playa Hermosa	1st.	Malecón Atacames	731518
Azul Pacífico	2nd.	Vía a Atacames	731203
Latinos	2nd.	Barrio Nueva Granada	731566
Cabañas:			
Arco Iris	1st.	Malecón Playas	731069
Le Castell	1st.	Malecón Playas	731542
Cocobamba	1st.	Junto al Cementerio	731303
Puerto Plata	1st.	Vía Atacames	731083
Caída del Sol	2nd.	Malecón del Río	731479
Cayapas	2nd.	Entrada a la Playa	731047
Juan Sebastián	2nd.	Malecón Playas	731049
La Aldea	2nd.	Entrada a la Playa	731424
Los Bohíos	2nd.	Entrada a la Playa	731089
Marbella	2nd.	Transversal Playa	731129
Nuevo Amanecer	2nd.	Malecón Playas	
Oasis de Siwua	2nd.	Luis Tello y Pasaje A	731347
Pensiones:			
Alta Gracia	2nd.	Entrada a la Playa	
Casa del Manglar	2nd.	Ingreso a la Playa	731464
Las Canarias	2nd.	Transversal de la Playa	710465
Sage	2nd.	Transversal Playa	731246
Apartamentos Turísticos:			
Jakara	1st.	Vía Súa	731065
La Marimba	1st.	Vía Súa	731412
Villa Solar	1st.	Barrio Nueva Granada	731428
El Pilar	2nd.	Barrio Nueva Granada	731462

CASTELNUOVO
Hostales Residencia:

La Tolita	2nd.	Playa Ancha	731249

Cabañas:

El Bosque	2nd.	Castelnuovo	731032
Jean Pierre	2nd.	Castelnuovo	731352

TONSUPA
Hostales:

Playa Ancha	1st.	Playa Ancha	731115
Tayta Raymi	1st.	Playa Ancha	731486
Costa de Oro	2nd.	Playa Ancha	731594
Delfín Dorado	2nd.	Playa Ancha	731177

Hosterías:

Cabo Blanco	1st.	Playa Ancha	731407
Caba Plan	1st.	Playa Ancha	731174
Club del Pacífico	1st.	Playa Ancha	731053
Puerto Ballesta	1st.	Playa Ancha	731538
Terrazas Washu	1st.	Playa Ancha	731358
Villa Rica	1st.	Playa Ancha	731420
Baños y Recreaciones	2nd.	Vía Atacames	710725
Italia	2nd.	Playa Ancha	731189
Playa Tonsupa	2nd.	San Carlos	731214

Cabañas:

Canaima Coral	1st.	San Carlos, Malecón	731172
D'Luis	1st.	Playa Ancha	731562
La Campiña	1st.	Playa Ancha	731371
La Chiquis	1st.	San Carlos, Malecón	731332
Las Palmeras	1st.	Playa Ancha	731443
Vista Azul	1st.	Playa Ancha	731175
Armenia	2nd.	Playa Ancha	710446
Caribe	2nd.	Playa Ancha	726387
El Sol Dorado	2nd.	Playa Ancha	
Espejo	2nd.	Playa Ancha	731554
Marcoli	2nd.	Entrada Playa Ancha	
Playa Azul	2nd.	Playa Ancha	321462
Torres Gemelas	2nd.	Playa Ancha	731219
Verde Mar	2nd.	Transversal Playa Ancha	332557

Pensiones:

Casa del Mar	2nd.	Playa Ancha, Malecón	
El Encuentro	2nd.	Playa Ancha, Malecón	731461
Miramar	2nd.	Playa Ancha, Malecón	731585

Apartamentos Turísticos:

Castelmar	1st.	Playa Ancha	731556
Tonsupa Suites	2nd.	Playa Ancha	731559

SÚA
Hoteles:

Chagra Ramos	2nd.	Playa de Súa, Malecón	713006

Hostales:

Bahía de Súa	2nd.	Malecón Súa	
Peñón de Súa	2nd.	Transversal Playa	731013
Shamán	2nd.	Malecón Súa	731486

Cabañas:

Los Jardines	2nd.	Entrada a Súa	506939
Marimar	2nd.	Entrada a Súa	
Oasis	2nd.	Transversal Playa	731310

SAME
Hosterías:

El Acantilado	2nd.	Km. 39 vía Muisne	453606

Cabañas:

Islas del Sol	1st.	Malecón	731151

Ciudades Vacacionales:

Marraquech	1st.	Playa	731298

MUISNE
Hostales Residencia:

Galápagos	2nd.	Transversal Playa	780758

SAN LORENZO
Hostales:

Carondelet	2nd.	21 de Mayo e I. Ayora	780202
Gran San Carlos	2nd.	Imbabura y J. Garcés	780267

Hostales Residencia:

Imperial San Lorenzo	2nd.	Imbabura y 10 de Agosto	780242

Pensiones:

Continental	2nd.	Imbabura	780126

BORBÓN
Pensiones:

Posada Esteban	2nd.	Río Cayapas	

CAMARONES
Cabañas:

La Fragata	2nd.	Av. Principal	

QUININDÉ
Hostales Residencia:

Sans	2nd.	6 de Diciembre	736522

Pensiones:

Cavendich	2nd.	Vía Esmeraldas	736872

MANABÍ

PORTOVIEJO **(05)**
Hoteles:

Casa Blanca	1st.	Km. 2.5 vía Crucita	634561
Ejecutivo	1st.	18 de Octubre	632385
New York	1st.	Francisco P. Moreira	632037
Cabrera Internacional	2nd.	García Moreno y P. Gual	633199
Hoteles Residencia:			
La Estancia	1st.	Av. del Ejército	931844
Colón	2nd.	Colón y Olmedo	630812
Conquistador	2nd.	18 de Octubre	651472
Madrid	2nd.	García Moreno y P. Gual	631326
San Marco	2nd.	Olmedo y 9 de Octubre	630650
Hoteles Apartamento:			
Don Juan	2nd.	Km. 3 vía Manta	931710
Los Vergeles	2nd.	Km. 10 vía Manta	
Hostales:			
Barandhúa	1st.	Malecón y Av. Deportista	676159
California	1st.	Ciudadela California	634415
El Gato	1st.	Pedro Gual y Olmedo	636908
Rey David	2nd.	Malecón Norte	
Sol Alondra	2nd.	José Castro y Malecón	
Cabañas:			
Quito	2nd.	San José y calle principal	

MANTA
Hoteles:

Haddad Manabí Hotel	1st.	Malecón, calle 102	622710
Las Gaviotas	1st.	Malecón de Tarqui 1100	620140
Manta Imperial	1st.	Playa del Murciélago	612806
Barbasquilo	2nd.	Final 4ta. Barbasquilo	620718
El Inca	2nd.	Av. 105 y Malecón	620440
Las Rocas	2nd.	Av. 105 y calle 101	612856
Lun Fun	2nd.	Av. 11 y calle 2	622966
Panorama Inn	2nd.	Calle 103 y Av. 105	611552
Hoteles Apartamento:			
Oasis	2nd.	Vía Manta-Rocafuerte	920680
Hostales:			
María José	1st.	La 29 y Av. F. Reyes	612294

BAHÍA DE CARÁQUEZ
Hoteles:

Italia	1st.	Av. Bolívar	691137
La Herradura	1st.	Av. Bolívar	690446
La Piedra	1st.	Av. Circunvalación	691473
Bahía Hotel	2nd.	Malecón y Vinueza	690823
Hostales:			
Bahía bed and breakfast	2nd.	Ascázubi 314	690146
La Querencia	2nd.	Malecón y H. Santos	690009
Hosterías:			
Quinta W	1st.	Km. 8 vía Chone	691386
Pensiones:			
Casa Grande	1st.	Av. Virgilio Ratty	692008

CHONE
Hoteles:

Atahualpa de Oro	1st.	Atahualpa y Páez	696697
Hostales:			
Chonanas	2nd.	Washington y Atahualpa	695236
Chone	2nd.	Pichincha y Páez	695064
Los Naranjos	2nd.	Washington y Pichincha	695451

JIPIJAPA
Hostales:

Hostal Jipijapa	2nd.	Santiesteban y E. Alfaro	601635

SAN JACINTO

Hostales:

Las Acacias	2nd.	Vía Laboratorios	
San Jacinto	2nd.	Av. Quito	

SAN VICENTE

Hostales:

El Montes	2nd.	Peatonal s/n y Malecón	674201

Pensiones:

Teresita	2nd.	Malecón	

Cabañas:

Alcatraz	1st.	Malecón	674179
Las Hamacas	1st.	Malecón, vía Canoa	674134
Monte Mar	1st.	Malecón	674197

GUAYAS

GUAYAQUIL **(04)**

Hoteles:

Continental	Lux.	Chile 510 y 10 de Agosto	329270
Grand Hotel Guayaquil	Lux.	Boyacá y C. Ballén	329690
Hilton Colón Internac.	Lux.	Cdla. Kennedy Norte	689000
Oro Verde	Lux.	García M. y 9 de Octubre	327999
Ramada	Lux.	Malecón y Orellana	565555
Sol de Oriente	Lux.	Aguirre 603 y Escobedo	325550
Unipark	Lux.	Clemente Ballén 406	327100
Alexander	1st.	Luque 1107 y P. Moncayo	532000
Del Rey	1st.	Aguirre y Andrés Marín	450971
Doral	1st.	Chile 402 y Aguirre	327171
Indira	1st.	García Avilés 101	310606
Las Américas	1st.	Machala 811	690883
Los Andes	1st.	Lorenzo de Garaycoa1233	329741
Orquídea No. 2	1st.	Av. Olmedo 309 y Chile	406970
Palace	1st.	Chile 216 y Luque	321080
Plaza	1st.	Chile 414 y C. Ballén	327140
Presidente	1st.	Chile 303 y Luque	531300
Ritz	1st.	9 de Octubre 709	324134
Rizzo	1st.	Clemente Ballén 319	325210
Andy	2nd.	V. Manuel Rendón 819	311666
California	2nd.	Ximena 601 y Urdaneta	302538
Capri	2nd.	Luque 1221	326341
Caribe	2nd.	Av. Olmedo 250 y Chile	526162
Centenario	2nd.	Vélez 726 y L. Garaycoa	524467
Colonial	2nd.	L. Urdaneta 534	303493
María del Cisne	2nd.	Chiriboga 204	
Mirasol	2nd.	Cooperativa C. del Cóndor	533811
Nevada	2nd.	L. de Garaycoa 710	304579
Niucanche	2nd.	P. Montúfar y Aguirre	512312
Nuevo Ecuador	2nd.	P. Moncayo 1117	321460
Plaza Centenario	2nd.	Lorenzo de Garaycoa 728	515578
Regina	2nd.	Lorenzo de Garaycoa 423	312754
Reina Victoria	2nd.	E. Moncayo 1135	
Tres Estrellas	2nd.	Cuenca y la Octava	366108

Hoteles Residencia:

Mi Casa	2nd.	Primero de Mayo 1010	285099

Hoteles Apartamento:

Apartamentos Boulevard	Lux.	9 de Octubre 432	566660
Suites El Ejecutivo	1st.	Escobedo 1403 y Luque	329180

Hostales:

Acuario	1st.	Luque 1204 y Quito	533715
La Concordia	1st.	9 de Octubre 1703	321726
Paseo Real	1st.	Luque 1009	513317

Pensiones:

De Alborada	2nd.	Alborada, Etapa 4	237251
El Paraíso	2nd.	4 de Noviembre 2715	

SALINAS

Hoteles:

Don Mincho	2nd.	Carretera Libertad-Salinas	775543
Las Conchas	2nd.	Cdla. Las Conchas	775937
Oasis	2nd.	Calle 44 entre Av. 20, 21	772473
Salinas	2nd.	Gral. Enríquez Gallo	772179
Salinas Costa Azul	2nd.	27 y Gral. Enríquez Gallo	774280

Hoteles Apartamento:

Calypso 1	1st.	Malecón de Salinas	772425

Hostales:

El Carruaje	1st.	Malecón 517	774282

El Tropikal	1st.	Calle 38 y Av. Tercera	773338
Albita	2nd.	Av. 7 y calle 23	773211
Cantábrico	2nd.	Av. 2 y Eloy Alfaro	772026
Florida	2nd.	Malecón y calle 2	772780
Italiana	2nd.	Cdla. Italiana, calle 54	777199
Palacio del Mar	2nd.	Av. 25 y calle 33	774144
Yulee	2nd.	Sector Chipipe	772028
Pensiones:			
Sol Mar	1st.	Av. 31 entre la 32 y 34	773214
Carloncho	2nd.	Av. 2 y Malecón	773194
Cabañas:			
El Reposo del Guerrero	2nd.	Calle 53 y Av. 43	776134
LIBERTAD			
Hoteles:			
Samarina	1st.	9 de Octubre y Malecón	785167
Collins Cabrera	2nd.	Diagonal Segunda 715	784241
Las Bahamas	2nd.	Av. 12 de Octubre	785860
Palatino	2nd.	Guayaquil y calle 4	786770
Hoteles Apartamento:			
Valdivia Club	1st.	Costa Azul, fase 3	775144
Hostales:			
Viña del Mar	2nd.	Guayaquil y Av. Tercera	785979
PUNTA CARNERO			
Hoteles:			
Punta Carnero	Lux.	Punta Carnero	775450
Del Mar	1st.	Punta Carnero	775370
Hosterías:			
Puerto Aguaje	1st.	Punta Carnero	
BALLENITA			
Hoteles:			
Farallón Dillon	1st.	Lomas de Ballenita	785611
Ballenita Inn	2nd.	Entrada a Ballenita	758008
SANTA ELENA			
Hoteles Apartamento:			
Costa Mar	1st.	Km. 7 vía Punta Blanca	560801
Hostales:			
El Cisne	2nd.	Sucre y Guayaquil	740038
MANGLARALTO			
Hoteles:			
Baja Montañita	1st.	Recinto Baja Montañita	901219
Hosterías:			
Las Olas	1st.	Vía Manglaralto	785707
EL TRIUNFO			
Hoteles:			
El Triunfo	2nd.	Av. Principal	724213
Hostales:			
Bulubulu	2nd.	A. Bucaram, principal	724269
MILAGRO			
Hosterías:			
La Higuera	2nd.	Km. 25 vía Durán-Tambo	565634
Pensiones:			
Milagro	2nd.	9 de Octubre y G. Moreno	
PLAYAS			
Hoteles:			
Bellavista	1st.	Km. 2 vía Data	760600
El Tucano	1st.	Km. 1.5 vía Data	760127
Los Parasoles	2nd.	Paquisha y A. Jurado	760532
Playas	2nd.	Malecón y Jambelí	760121
Hostales:			
Oro Azul	1st.	Sixto Casin y Pública	760704
Acapulco	2nd.	Malecón y Av. J. Roldós	
Cattan	2nd.	3 de Noviembre y Jambelí	760174
El Delfín	2nd.	Km. 1 vía Data	760125
El Galeón	2nd.	15 de Agosto	760270
Las Redes	2nd.	Km. 7 vía Data	760222
Reina del Mar	2nd.	Av. Roldós y Malecón	760882
Rey David	2nd.	Novena y Av. Primera	760024
Sol y Mar	2nd.	Malecón Jambelí	760777
Hosterías:			
Los Patios	1st.	Km. 1.5 vía Data	760039
El Pinar	2nd.	Km. 4.5 vía Data	760051

LOS RÍOS

BABAHOYO **(05)**

Hoteles:			
Cachari	2nd.	Bolívar 111 y Gral. Barona	734443
Emperador	2nd.	G. Barona y 27 de Mayo	732512
Hoteles Apartamento:			
Almendros	2nd.	Cdla. La Alvira	
Hostales:			
Riveras de Babahoyo	2nd.	Malecón y Pedro Carbo	
QUEVEDO			
Hoteles:			
Olímpico	1st.	Cdla. San José	750210
Quevedo Internacional	1st.	7 de Octubre	751876
Ejecutivo	2nd.	7 de Octubre y la Cuarta	
Rancho San Vinicio	2nd.	Km. 2 vía Valencia	751876
Hoteles Apartamento:			
El Jardín	2nd.	Km. 6 vía Empalme	
Hostales:			
Central	2nd.	Bolívar y la Novena	750701
Continental	2nd.	7 de Octubre y la Octava	750080
Flor de Líbano	2nd.	Bolívar 928 y la Décima	755500
Hilton	2nd.	Progreso y la Novena	751359
Mi Casa Blanca	2nd.	Décima 412	754144

EL ORO

MACHALA **(07)**

Hoteles:			
Inés	1st.	Juan Montalvo 1509	
Montecarlo	1st.	Guayas y Olmedo	933104
Oro Hotel	1st.	Sucre y Juan Montalvo	932408
Perla del Pacífico	1st.	Sucre 613 y Páez	930915
Rizzo	1st.	Guayas y Bolívar	921511
San Francisco Internac.	1st.	Tarqui y Sucre	938506
Araujo	2nd.	9 de Mayo y Boyacá	935257
Ecuatoriano Pullman	2nd.	9 de Octubre y Colón	930197
Mosquera	2nd.	Olmedo y Guayas	930392
Pacífico	2nd.	Gral. Páez 244, P. Bolívar	920328
Hostales:			
Edison	1st.	Boyacá y Colón	938120
El Ejecutivo	1st.	Sucre y 9 de Mayo	
Bolívar	2nd.	Municipalidad y Apolinario	
El Alcázar	2nd.	Las Palmeras	935577
Julio César	2nd.	9 de Mayo y Boyacá	937978
La Bahía	2nd.	Olmedo y Junín	
Mercy	2nd.	Junín y Sucre	920116
Molina	2nd.	Pasaje y J. Montalvo	938365
Patty	2nd.	Boyacá 619 y Ayacucho	931759
Salinas	2nd.	Arízaga y 10 de Agosto	934702
EL GUABO			
Hostales:			
El Turista	2nd.	3 de Noviembre y la B	
HUAQUILLAS			
Hoteles:			
Lima	2nd.	Portovelo y Machala	907262
Hostales:			
Vanessa	1st.	1 de Mayo y Av. Hualtaco	907263
Alameda	2nd.	Tnte. Cordovéz 331	
Rodey	2nd.	Tnte. Cordovéz	907736
JAMBELÍ			
Hostales:			
María Sol	2nd.	Malecón s/n	937461
Cabañas:			
Cabaña del Pescador	2nd.	Jambelí	
PASAJE			
Hostales:			
Cordillera	2nd.	Colón y Eloy Alfaro	
Internacional	2nd.	Ochoa León y Azuay	
San Martín	2nd.	Bolívar y Olmedo	
Wimper	2nd.	Juan Montalvo	
Hosterías:			
San Luis	2nd.	Km. 4 vía Cuenca	910904
Pensiones:			
El Ejecutivo	2nd.	Municipalidad 419	911533

PIÑAS

Hoteles:

La Orquídea	2nd.	Abdón Calderón s/n	

SANTA ROSA

Hoteles:

América	1st.	El Oro y Sucre	
Santa Rosa	2nd.	Colón y Vega Dávila	

CARCHI

TULCÁN **(06)**

Hoteles:

Azteca	1st.	Bolívar y Atahualpa	981447
Rumichaca	1st.	PuenteInter. Rumichaca	980276
Sáenz Internacional	1st.	Sucre y Rocafuerte	983925
Torres de Oro Internac.	1st.	Sucre y Rocafuerte	980296

Hoteles Residencia:

Quillasinga	2nd.	Sucre y Ayacucho	981892

Hostales:

Machado	1st.	Ayacucho 403 y Bolívar	984221
Los Alpes	2nd.	J.R. Arellano y Veintimilla	982235

Hostales Residencia:

Alejandra	2nd.	Sucre y Quito	981784
Casa Grande	2nd.	Colón y Chimborazo	983433
España	2nd.	Sucre y Pje. La Concordia	983860
Oasis	2nd.	10 de Agosto 6031	980342
Sucre	2nd.	Junín y Bolívar	

IMBABURA

IBARRA **(06)**

Hoteles:

Ajaví	1st.	Av. Mariano Acosta 16-38	955225
La Casona de los Lagos	1st.	Sucre 3-50 y Grijalva	957844
La Giralda	1st.	Av. Atahualpa y J. Bonilla	956002
Montecarlo	1st.	Av. J. Rivadeneira 563	958266
Turismo Internacional	1st.	Rafael Troya	956331
El Conquistador	2nd.	Autopista Yaguarcocha	640780

Hoteles Residencia:

Madrid No. 2	2nd.	Pedro Moncayo 7-41	956177

Hostales:

Blue Lake	2nd.	Pedro Moncayo y Bolívar	641851
El Dorado	2nd.	Oviedo 541 y Sucre	950699
Ecuador	2nd.	Obpo. Mosquera 554	956425
Imbaya Real	2nd.	Pedro Moncayo 744	959729
Nueva Colonia	2nd.	Olmedo 519 y Grijalva	952918

Hostales Residencia:

El Ejecutivo	2nd.	Bolívar 9-69 y Colón	956575

Hosterías:

Chorlaví	1st.	Panamericana Sur km. 5	932222
El Prado	1st.	Panamericana Norte km. 1	959570
El Rancho de Carolina	1st.	Panamericana Sur km. 5	955215
Rancho Totoral	1st.	Autopista Yaguarcocha	955544
San Alfonso de Moras	1st.	Panamericana Sur	932499
San Agustín	2nd.	Panamericana Sur km. 4	955888

Cabañas:

Mirador de Yaguarcocha	2nd.	La Victoria, El Olivo Alto	951736

Pensiones:

Madrid No. 1	2nd.	Olmedo 8-57	951760

Paradores:

Yaguarcocha	2nd.	Autopista Yaguarcocha	951500

AMBUQUÍ

Hosterías:

Aruba	1st.	Panam. Norte km. 36.5	941114
El Edén del Valle	2nd.	Panam. Norte km. 32	941116
El Jordán	2nd.	Panam. Norte km. 39	941112
El Oasis	2nd.	Panam. Norte km. 35	941200
Tierra del Sol	2nd.	Panam. Norte km. 35	

ANTONIO ANTE

Hostales:

Imbabura Real	2nd.	Bolívar y Amazonas	911542

COTACACHI

Hostales:

Jora Continental	2nd.	Sucre 4-76 y S. Moreno	915169
Primitivo	2nd.	Entrada Ramal Panam.	915928

Hosterías:

La Banda	1st.	Av. 10 de Agosto 2283	915873
La Mirage	1st.	Av. 10 de Agosto	915237
Mesón de las Flores	1st.	García Moreno y Sucre	915009

ILUMÁN

Hosterías:

Hcda. Pinsaquí	1st.	Panam. Norte km. 5	920387

NATABUELA

Hosterías:

Natabuela	1st.	Panamericana Sur km. 8	955755

OTAVALO

Hoteles:

El Indio	1st.	Bolívar 904 y A. Calderón	920325
Yamor Continental	1st.	Av. Luis Ponce de León	920451
Otavalo	2nd.	Roca 5-04 y J. Montalvo	920416

Hoteles Residencia:

El Coraza	2nd.	A. Calderón y Sucre	921225

Hostales:

Ali Shungu	2nd.	Quito y Miguel Egas	920750
Doña Esther	2nd.	Juan Montalvo 444	920739
Inca Real	2nd.	Salinas y Sucre	922895
Pacari	2nd.	Cdla. 31 de Octubre	922169
Rincón de Belén	2nd.	Roca y Juan Montalvo	920171

Hostales Residencia:

Centenario	2nd.	Pasaje Saona 703	920467
Curaca Real	2nd.	31 de Octubre y Quito	922438

Hosterías:

La Casa de Laredo	1st.	Prolongación Sucre 11-99	920443

Pensiones:

San Sebastián	2nd.	Roca 9-05 y Morales	920208

SAN ANTONIO DE IBARRA

Hosterías:

Marthy Zu	2nd.	Vía San Lorenzo	910636

SAN PABLO

Hostales:

Chicapán	2nd.	Orillas Lago San Pablo	920331

Hosterías:

Cabañas del Lago	1st.	Orillas Lago San Pablo	918001
Cusín	1st.	Hacienda Cusín	918013
Puerto Lago	1st.	Panam. Sur km. 5.5	920900

URCUQUÍ

Hosterías:

San Francisco	1st.	Km. 19 vía Chachimbiro	920387

PICHINCHA

QUITO **(02)**

Hoteles:

Akros	Lux.	Av. 6 de Diciembre 3986	430600
Alameda Real	Lux.	Roca y Av. Amazonas	562345
Crowne Plaza	Lux.	Av. Los Shyris 1757	445305
Hilton Colón Internac.	Lux.	Avs. Amazonas y Patria	560666
Oro Verde	Lux.	Av. 12 de Octubre 1820	566497
Quito	Lux.	Av. González Suárez 2500	540600
Radisson	Lux.	Cordero y Av. 12 de Oct.	229226
Alejandro	1st.	Av. 10 de Agosto 1976	247196
Ambassador	1st.	9 de Octubre y Av. Colón	561777
Auca Continental	1st.	Sucre 530 y Venezuela	512240
Chalet Suisse	1st.	Reina Victoria y Calama	562700
Dan	1st.	Av. 10 de Agosto y Colón	553745
Embassy	1st.	Wilson 441	561990
Inca imperial	1st.	Bogotá 219 y Salinas	524800
Real Audiencia	1st.	Bolívar 220 y Guayaquil	512711
Reina Isabel	1st.	Av. Amazonas 842	226040
República	1st.	Av. República y Azuay	436553
Saint	1st.	El Comercio 115 y El Día	246114
Santa María	1st.	Inglaterra 933	562428
Savoy Inn	1st.	Yasuní 304 y Av. El Inca	460620
Sebastián	1st.	Diego de Almagro 822	222400
Seis de Diciembre	1st.	Av. 6 de Diciembre 1230	544863
Tambo Real	1st.	Av. 12 de Octubre	544970
Zumag	1st.	Nueva Orleans 224	552400
Alstong Inn	2nd.	Juan León Mera 741	222721
Complejo Amazonas	2nd.	Maldonado 915	611355
Coral Internacional	2nd.	Manuel Larrea 164	572237

Cumandá	2nd.	Morales 449	516984
G.D. Oro	2nd.	Santa Rosa 436 y Armero	543033
Grand Hotel	2nd.	Rocafuerte 1001 y Pontón	519411
Intern. Plaza del Teatro	2nd.	Guayaquil 1363	514293
Majestic	2nd.	Mercadillo 366	546388
9 de Octubre	2nd.	9 de Octubre 1047	525715
Quito Palace	2nd.	18 de Septiembre 1117	566214
Santa Clara Internac.	2nd.	Gustavo Darquea 1578	541472
Versalles	2nd.	Versalles 1442	526145
Viena Internacional	2nd.	Flores 610 y Chile	519611
Hoteles Residencia:			
Dorado No. 2	2nd.	18 de Septiembre 805	230903
Juana de Arco	2nd.	Rocafuerte 1311	214175
Piedra Dorada	2nd.	Maldonado 3210	517460
Hoteles Apartamento:			
Amaranta	1st.	Leonidas Plaza 194	560585
American Suites	1st.	Av. Eloy Alfaro 3333	461779
Colón	1st.	Leonidas Plaza 326	563244
Mariscal	1st.	Robles 958 y Valdivia	528833
Hostales:			
Baraka	1st.	Asunción 567	509280
Barnard	1st.	Queseras del Medio 598	540629
Camila's	1st.	Av. 6 de Diciembre 1329	225412
Carrión	1st.	Carrión 1250 y Versalles	234620
Casa Blanca	1st.	Asunción 141	221129
Cumbres	1st.	Baquedano 148	560850
El Portón	1st.	San Javier 203	234289
El Príncipe	1st.	América 660 y Asunción	543795
El Relicario	1st.	Reina Victoria 1714	552528
Floresta	1st.	Isabel La Católica 1015	523508
Ibiza	1st.	Brasil 455 y Azcúnaga	457169
Jardín Quiteño	1st.	Versalles 1449	526011
Koronado	1st.	Luis Cordero 779	565643
La Carolina	1st.	Italia 324 y Vancouver	542473
La Casona	1st.	Manabí 251 y Flores	514764
La Fragata	1st.	Mosquera Narváez 269	226190
La Pradera	1st.	San Salvador 222	226833
La Villa de Toledo	1st.	Toledo 1455	222755
Los Alpes	1st.	Tamayo 233	561110
Los Andes	1st.	Muros 146	550839
Palm Garten	1st.	9 de Octubre y Cordero	523960
Plaza Internacional	1st.	Leonidas Plaza 150	524530
Posada Real	1st.	Plácido Caamaño 213	552511
Reino de Quito	1st.	Maldonado 2648	510347
Rincón Escandinavo	1st.	Leonidas Plaza 1110	222168
Roland's	1st.	Italia 241 y Vancouver	563645
Santa Bárbara	1st.	Av. 12 de Octubre 2263	225123
Sierra Nevada	1st.	Pinto 637 y Cordero	553653
Vizcaya	1st.	Rumipamba 1716	452252
Aeropuerto	2nd.	Av. Amazonas 7955	458708
Belmonte	2nd.	Antepara 413 y León	516235
Café Cultura	2nd.	Robles 513	224271
El Balcón	2nd.	Río de Janeiro 201	225511
El Batán	2nd.	Av. 6 de Diciembre 5141	250874
Farget	2nd.	Pasaje Farget 109	570066
Pikcett	2nd.	Wilson 712	551205
Rincón de Bavaria	2nd.	Páez 232 y 18 de Sept.	509401
Román	2nd.	Tomás de Berlanga 537	248289
Viena	2nd.	Tamayo 879 y Foch	235413
Hostales Residencia:			
Catedral Internacional	1st.	Mejía 638 y Benalcázar	515438
Charles Darwin	1st.	La Colina 304	529384
Jazmín	1st.	Av. Amazonas 232	523615
Las Cibeles	1st.	Isla Floreana 726	451288
Taurino	1st.	Av. Amazonas 5444	441656
Terrazas Suites	1st.	Isla San Cristóbal 880	259620
Villantigua	1st.	Jorge Washington 237	227018
Pensiones:			
La Coupole	1st.	Roca 518	508912
La Estancia	1st.	Wilson 508 y Almagro	235993
La Rábida	1st.	La Rábida 227	222169
La Rinconada	1st.	Isla Genovesa 673	249981
Los Maderos	1st.	Pedro Basán	241893
Madrid 868	1st.	Madrid 868	554621

CONOCOTO

Hoteles:

Castillo del Valle	1st.	Av. Ilaló 2039	320965

CUMBAYÁ

Hoteles:

Brandemburg	1st.	San Juan Alto	890187

GUAYLLABAMBA

Hoteles:

Guayllabamba	1st.	Huertos Familiares	361679
María José	1st.	Panam. Norte	363139

PUEMBO

Hosterías:

San José	1st.	Rafael Burbano s/n	390264

SAN RAFAEL

Hostales:

Del Valle	1st.	Urb. Armenia 1-12	341196
Holiday	2nd.	La Y, vía El Tingo	321085

SANGOLQUÍ

Hosterías:

Mansión Samzara	1st.	Barrio Santa Clara	361291
Sommergarten	1st.	Chimborazo 248 y Riofrío	330315

CAYAMBE

Hosterías:

Casa Vieja Guachalá	1st.	Panam. Norte km. 70	224149
Las Cabañas de Nápoles	1st.	Panam. Norte km. 1.5	360366
Mitad del Mundo	2nd.	Av. Natalia Jarrín	360226
El Rancho	2nd.	Panam. Norte km. 1.5	360321

NONO

Hosterías:

San Jorge	1st.	Camino a Nono km. 5	545964

SANTO DOMINGO DE LOS COLORADOS

Hoteles:

Zaracay	Lux.	Av. Quito 1639	750316
Don Kléber	1st.	Km. 2 vía Esmeraldas	761243
El Marqués	1st.	Km. 4 vía Quevedo	753292
Tropical Inn	1st.	Km. 2 vía Quito	761771
El Colorado	2nd.	Av. 29 de Mayo	750226
Diana Real	2nd.	Loja y 29 de Mayo	751380
Toachi	2nd.	Av. Quito, km. 1.5	754688

Hoteles Residencia:

Ejecutivo No. 2	2nd.	29 de Mayo y Ambato	763305

Hostales:

Acuarius	1st.	Av. Quevedo km. 1	750015
Aracely	2nd.	Vía Quevedo y San Miguel	
Descanso del Conduc.	2nd.	Km. 4.5 vía Quevedo	754418
La Caleta	2nd.	Ibarra 141 y 29 de Mayo	750277
La Finca	2nd.	Km. 2 vía Quinindé	761249
Rey	2nd.	Av. Chone	753489
Siesta	2nd.	Av. Quito 1277	751013

Hostales Residencia:

Amancay	2nd.	Av. 29 de Mayo y Ambato	750696
Ejecutivo	2nd.	Av. 29 de Mayo 520	751943
Génova	2nd.	Ibarra y 29 de Mayo	750277
La Fuente Azul	2nd.	Caminos Vecinales MOP	759690
Los Ángeles	2nd.	Lotización Los Ángeles	
Lucy	2nd.	Av. Quito	750263
Patricia	2nd.	Abraham Calazacón	761906
Príncipe Real	2nd.	Ambato 410 y Manta	750492

Hosterías:

La Hacienda	1st.	Km. 13 vía Chone	750356
Los Colorados	1st.	Km. 12 vía Quito	753449
Mi Cuchito	1st.	Km. 2 vía Chone	750636
Valle Hermoso	1st.	Km. 25 vía Esmeraldas	773208

Pensiones:

Gabriela	2nd.	Machala 385	
Los Ceibos	2nd.	Abraham Calazacón	
Núñez	2nd.	Esmeraldas y Tiputini	

COTOPAXI

LATACUNGA **(03)**

Hostales:

Rodelu	1st.	Quito 7331 y P. Salcedo	811264
Central	2nd.	Sánchez de Orellana	802912

Cotopaxi	2nd.	Sánchez de Orellana 721	801310
Quilotoa	2nd.	Av. Eloy Alfaro y Andrade	800099
LASSO			
Hosterías:			
La Ciénega	1st.	Hcda. La Ciénega	719093
LA MANÁ			
Hosterías:			
Inmisau	1st.	Vía La Maná-Quevedo	688281
SALCEDO			
Hoteles:			
Del Río	1st.	Hcda. San Luis	
Hosterías:			
Rumipamba de las Rosas	1st.	Panam. Sur km. 100	726128
		TUNGURAHUA	
AMBATO			**(03)**
Hoteles:			
Ambato	1st.	Rocafuerte y Guayaquil	827598
De las Flores	1st.	Av. El Rey y Mul Mul	851424
Florida	1st.	Av. Miraflores 1131	823040
Miraflores	1st.	Av. Miraflores	843224
Villa Hilda	1st.	Av. Miraflores y Las Lilas	845571
Bellavista	2nd.	Oriente y Napo Pastaza	847535
Ejecutivo	2nd.	12 de Noviembre 1230	840370
San Ignacio	2nd.	Maldonado y 12 de Nov.	824370
Tungurahua	2nd.	Av. Cevallos 1834	823585
Hostales:			
Colonial	1st.	Luis A. Martínez y Sucre	827134
Gran Hotel	1st.	Rocafuerte y Lalama	824235
Pirámide Inn	1st.	Av. Cevallos y M. Egüez	825252
Señorial	1st.	Av. Cevallos y Quito	825244
Imperial	2nd.	12 de Noviembre 2492	844837
Portugal	2nd.	Juan Cajas 005	823218
Hostales Residencia:			
Cevallos	1st.	Av. Cevallos y Montalvo	847437
La Pradera	1st.	Av. Los Chasquis	827913
BAÑOS			
Hoteles:			
Sangay	1st.	Plaza Isidro Ayora	740490
Flor de Oriente	2nd.	Ambato y Maldonado	740418
Palace	2nd.	Montalvo 20-03	740470
Hostales:			
Achupallas	2nd.	16 de Diciembre	740389
Casa Real	2nd.	Montalvo y Sta. Clara	740215
Isla de Baños	2nd.	T. Alflants y Montalvo	740609
Los Andes	2nd.	Oriente 118 y E. Alfaro	740838
Santa Cruz	2nd.	16 de Diciem. y Montalvo	740648
Villa Gertrudis	2nd.	Montalvo 419	740441
Hostales Residencia:			
Casa Blanca	2nd.	Oriente y Maldonado	740092
Charvic	2nd.	Maldonado y Oriente	740298
Magdalena	2nd.	Oriente 1047 y E. Alfaro	740233
Monick's	2nd.	Ambato y Pastaza	740428
Villa Santa Clara	2nd.	12 de Noviembre	740349
Pensiones:			
Casa Nahuazo	2nd.	Vía El Salado	740315
Cultura	2nd.	J. Montalvo y Sta. Clara	740419
El Marqués	2nd.	Av. Montalvo	740503
Le Petit Auberge	2nd.	E. Alfaro 246	740936
		CHIMBORAZO	
RIOBAMBA			**(03)**
Hoteles:			
Chimborazo Internac.	1st.	Los Nogales y Argentinos	963475
El Cisne	1st.	Av. Daniel León Borja	964573
El Galpón	1st.	Argentinos y C. Zambrano	960981
Manabí	2nd.	Colón 1958 y Olmedo	967967
Zeus	2nd.	Av. Daniel León Borja	968036
Hostales:			
El Altar	1st.	Panam. Norte km. 1	964872
Glamour	1st.	Primera Constituyente	962292
Montecarlo	1st.	10 de Agosto 2541	960557
Riobamba Inn	1st.	Carabobo 2320	961696
Humboldt	2nd.	Av. Daniel León Borja	961788

Los Álamos	2nd.	St. Aman Montrond	967386
Patricia	2nd.	Luis A. Falconí 3757	961525
Tren Dorado	2nd.	Carabobo 22-35	964890
Whymper	2nd.	Miguel A. León	964455
Hostales Residencia:			
Imperial	2nd.	Rocafuerte 2215	960429
Los Nevados	2nd.	Luis A. Costales 2437	964696
Los Shyris	2nd.	Rocafuerte 2160	960323
Rocío	2nd.	Brasil 2168	961848
Hosterías:			
Abraspungu	1st.	Km. 3 vía Guano	940820
Estancia Real	1st.	Km. 5 vía Chambo	969835
La Andaluza	1st.	Chuquipogyo, km. 16	904223
El Toril	1st.	Km. 2 vía Baños	942057
El Troje	1st.	Km. 4.5 vía Chambo	964572
PALLATANGA			
Hoteles:			
El Valle	2nd.	Vía Principal, km. 2	242216

BOLÍVAR

GUARANDA			**(03)**
Hostales:			
La Colina	1st.	Av. Guayaquil 103	980666
Cochapamba	1st.	García M. y 7 de Mayo	981958
BALZAPAMBA			
Hoteles:			
Cascada Milagrosa	2nd.	Km. 64 vía Babahoyo	656726

CAÑAR

AZOGUES			**(07)**
Hostales:			
Charles No. 2	2nd.	Serrano y Emilio Abad	241883
CAÑAR			
Hostales:			
Ingapirca	2nd.	Sucre 8-11	235201
LA TRONCAL			
Hoteles:			
Su Majestad	2nd.	Av. Principal, vía Durán	722140
Hostales:			
California	1st.	Av. Central s/n	722256
Hosterías:			
La Merced	1st.	Recinto Voluntad de Dios	722100

AZUAY

CUENCA			**(07)**
Hoteles:			
El Dorado	Lux.	Gran Colombia 7-87	831390
Oro Verde	Lux.	Av. Ordóñez Lasso s/n	832849
Alli Tiana	1st.	Presidente Córdova	821950
Atahualpa	1st.	Sucre 3-50	826906
Catedral	1st.	Padre Aguirre 8-17	823204
Conquistador	1st.	Gran Colombia 6-65	831788
Crespo	1st.	Calle Larga 7-93	834937
El Príncipe	1st.	J. Jaramillo 8-82	821235
Inca Real	1st.	Gral. Torres 8-40	823636
Italia	1st.	Sucre 6-78	827118
Pinar del Lago	1st.	Av. Ordóñez Lasso s/n	837339
Presidente	1st.	Gran Colombia 6-59	831066
Tomebamba	1st.	Bolívar 11-19	823997
Cuenca	2nd.	Av. España 1-29	831427
El Cisne	2nd.	Av. de las Américas s/n	881655
El Quijote	2nd.	Hermano Miguel 9-58	843197
Las Américas	2nd.	Mariano Cueva 13-59	831160
Los Libertadores	2nd.	Av. España 1-29	831427
Prado Inn	2nd.	Rocafuerte 3-45	807164
Tito	2nd.	Sangurima 1-49	829734
Hostales:			
Amazonas	1st.	Madrid y Aranjuez	839165
Bristol	1st.	Hurtado de Mendoza 1-48	861231
Casa Grande	1st.	Borrero 8-44	846916
Casas de Guapondelig	1st.	Guapondelig y J. Roldós	869117
Chordeleg	1st.	Gran Colombia 11-15	824611
Colonial	1st.	Gran Colombia 10-13	841644
Hurtado de Mendoza	1st.	Sangurima y H. Cápac	827909
Internacional	1st.	Benigno Malo 10-15	831348

La Orquídea	1st.	Borrero 9-31	823321
La Posada del Sol	1st.	Bolívar 5-03	838695
Caribe Inn	2nd.	Gran Colombia 10-51	835175
Hostales Residencia:			
Galeón Internacional	2nd.	Sangurima 2-42	831827
Paredes	2nd.	Luis Cordero 11-29	835674
París	2nd.	Gral. Torres 10-48	826656
Samay	2nd.	Tomás Ordóñez 11-86	831119
Siberia	2nd.	Luis Cordero 4-22	840672
Hosterías:			
Dos Chorreras	1st.	Km. 32 vía El Cajas	880200
El Molino	1st.	Panam. Norte km. 7	875367
Apartamentos Turísticos:			
Casa Bella	1st.	La República y del Retén	804397
Otorongo	1st.	Av. 12 de Abril y Guayas	811184
BAÑOS			
Hosterías:			
Durán	1st.	Parroquia Baños, km. 8	892486
GUALACEO			
Hosterías:			
Tambo La Rivera	1st.	Orillas Río Sta. Bárbara	
PAUTE			
Hosterías:			
Cabañas San Luis	1st.	Abdón Calderón s/n	250165
Hostería Uzhupud	1st.	Uzhupud, sector Chicán	250339
SANTA ISABEL			
Hosterías:			
La Molienda	1st.	Sector la Unión	270361
Sol y Agua	1st.	Sector la Unión	830325

LOJA

LOJA			**(07)**
Hoteles:			
Grand Hotel Loja	1st.	Av. Manuel A. Aguirre	571803
Libertador	1st.	Colón y Bolívar	572119
Ramses	1st.	Colón y Bolívar	561402
Saraguros Internac.	1st.	Av. Universitaria	570552
Vilcabamba	1st.	Av. Manuel A. Aguirre	573645
Hostales:			
Aguilera Internacional	1st.	Sucre y Emilio Ortega	563189
Inca	2nd.	Av. Universitaria	
Los Ejecutivos	2nd.	Av. Universitaria y Azuay	560004
Quiñara	2nd.	Av. Universitaria	570785
Riviera	2nd.	Av. Universitaria	573863
ALAMOR			
Hoteles:			
Grand Hotel Sica	2nd.	10 de Agosto y Colón	
MACARÁ			
Hostales:			
Espiga de Oro	2nd.	Antonio Anda	562476
Paradores Turísticos:			
Macará	1st.	Vía Panamericana	694099
VILCABAMBA			
Hosterías:			
Vilcabamba	1st.	Entrada a Vilcabamba	580271
Paradores Turísticos:			
Vilcabamba	1st.	Centro de Vilcabamba	673122
Cabañas:			
Madre Tierra	1st.	Entrada a Vilcabamba	580269
Paraíso	2nd.	Calle Eterna Juventud	
Pensiones:			
Posada Real	2nd.	Agua de Hierro	673114
Jardín Escondido	2nd.	Diego Vaca de Vega	580281
CATAMAYO			
Hosterías:			
Bellavista	2nd.	Trapichillo alto	677255

SUCUMBÍOS

NUEVA LOJA			**(06)**
Hoteles:			
Araza	1st.	Av. Quito 604	830223
El Cofán	1st.	12 de Febrero y Av. Quito	830527
D'Mario	2nd.	Av. Quito 171	830172

Hoteles Residencia:			
Palace	2nd.	Av. Amazonas	830458
Hostales:			
Americano	2nd.	Av. Quito 128	830555
Machala No. 2	2nd.	Av. Colombia 122	830073
San Jorge	2nd.	Barrio Guayaquil	830044
Sayonara	2nd.	Av. Quito y Gonzanamá	830562
Hostales Residencia:			
París	1st.	Jorge Añasco 146	830496
Shalon	2nd.	Av. Quito y El Chofer	831494
Hosterías:			
Gran Hostal del Lago	1st.	Av. Quito	830015
Cabañas:			
Amazon Jungle	1st.	Vía Tarapoa	834135
SHUSHUFINDI			
Hosterías:			
Amazonas	1st.	Vía El Pozo No. 9	839138
Cabañas:			
Sacha Lodge	1st.	Orillas Río Napo	522220

NAPO

TENA			**(06)**
Hostales:			
Auca	1st.	Vía Archidona	886461
Mol	1st.	Sucre 432	886215
Enmita	2nd.	Bolívar 447 y Montalvo	886253
Travellers Lodging	2nd.	15 de Noviembre 438	886372
Villa Belén	2nd.	Jumandy, barrio el Dorado	886228
Hostales Residencia:			
Alemana	2nd.	15 de Noviembre	886409
Caribe	2nd.	15 de Noviembre y Alfaro	886518
Hosterías:			
Los Yutzos	1st.	Augusto Rueda 190	886458
Pensiones:			
Turismo Amazónico	1st.	Amazonas y A. Calderón	886487
Danubio	2nd.	15 de Noviembre s/n	886378
Cabañas:			
Shangrila	2nd.	Km. 67 vía Puyo	886372
AHUANO			
Cabañas:			
Alizahui	1st.	Orillas del Río Napo	253267
La Casa del Suizo	1st.	Orillas del Río Napo	572164
Cotococha	1st.	Km. 10 vía Ahuano	541527
Jaguar	2nd.	Orillas del Río Napo	523779
Anaconda	2nd.	Isla Anaconda	886548
MISAHUALLÍ			
Hostales:			
Albergue Español	1st.	Juana Arteaga s/n	553857
Dayuma	1st.	Calle Principal	584964
Pensiones:			
La Posada	2nd.	Parque Central	
Cabañas:			
Jungle Lodge El Jardín	1st.	Vía Minas	522927
Misahuallí Jungle Hotel	1st.	Frente Puerto Misahuallí	520043
Dayuma	2nd.	Recinto Sta. Rosa de Puni	584965
Jungle Lodge Albergue	2nd.	Río Napo, Isla del Oro	553857
Txalaparta	2nd.	Vía Misahuallí	545131
ARCHIDONA			
Hostales Residencia:			
Regina	2nd.	Rocafuerte 446	889144
EL CHACO			
Hosterías:			
Los Yumbos	1st.	Vía Lago Agrio	536934
FRANCISCO DE ORELLANA			
Hoteles:			
La Misión	1st.	Frente a la M. Capuchina	880260
El Auca	2nd.	Napo y García Moreno	880600
Hostales:			
Oasis	2nd.	Vía La M. Capuchina	880164
Hostales Residencia:			
Amazonas	2nd.	Espejo y 12 de Febrero	880444
Cabañas:			
Oasis Yuturi	2nd.	Orillas Río Napo	880164

Panacocha	2nd.	Orillas Lag. Panacocha	565990
Hosterías:			
La Selva	1st.	Garzacocha	550995
Primavera	2nd.	Primavera Río Napo	
PUERTO NAPO			
Cabañas:			
Totococha	1st.	Puerto Napo, km. 10	541527

PASTAZA

PUYO			**(03)**
Hostales:			
Europa Internacional	1st.	9 de Octubre 1346	885228
Hostales Residencia:			
Araucano	2nd.	Ceslao Marín 576	885227
California	2nd.	9 de Octubre 1354	885189
Hosterías:			
Turingia	1st.	Ceslao Marín 294	885180
Orquídea Amazónica	2nd.	Km. 3 vía Puyo-Baños	883048
Safari	2nd.	Km. 5.5 vía Puyo-Tena	885466

MORONA SANTIAGO

MACAS			**(07)**
Hoteles:			
Peñón de Oriente	2nd.	Domingo Comín	700124
Hostales:			
La Orquídea	2nd.	9 de Octubre y Sucre	700970
Esmeraldas	2nd.	Cuenca y Soasty	
Splendit No. 1	2nd.	Soasty y D. Comín	700120
Hosterías:			
Cabañas del Valle	2nd.	Carretera Macas-Sucúa	

ZAMORA CHINCHIPE

ZAMORA			**(07)**
Hostales:			
Internacional Torres	2nd.	Francisco de Orellana	605195
Maguna	2nd.	Diego de Vega	

GALÁPAGOS

SANTA CRUZ			**(05)**
Hoteles:			
Palmeras	2nd.	Tomás de Berlanga	526139
Hostales:			
Angermeyer	1st.	Av. Charles Darwin	526188
Delfín	1st.	Barrio Estrada	526297
Galápagos	1st.	Av. Charles Darwin	526330
Las Ninfas	1st.	Los Colonos	526127
Castro	2nd.	Los Colonos	526113
Fernandina	2nd.	12 de Noviembre	526222
Fiesta	2nd.	Moisés Brito	526440
Lirio del Mar	2nd.	Bolívar Naveda	526212
Lobo de Mar	2nd.	12 de Febrero	526188
North Seymour	2nd.	Raúl Carrasco	526314
Nuevo Elizabeth	2nd.	Av. Charles Darwin	526178
Salinas	2nd.	Bolívar Naveda	526107
Pensiones:			
Solymar	1st.	Av. Charles Darwin	526281
España	2nd.	Tomás de Berlanga	526108
Estrella de Mar	2nd.	12 de Febrero	
SAN CRISTÓBAL			
Hostales:			
Flamingo	1st.	Ignacio de Hernández	
Galápagos Hostal	1st.	Sector Playa de Oro	520265
Northia	1st.	Av. Alsacio Northia s/n	520041
Orca	1st.	Sector Playa de Oro	520233
Cactus	2nd.	J. J. Flores	
Chatan	2nd.	Av. Armada Nacional s/n	520137
Mar Azul	2nd.	Av. Alsacio Northia s/n	520139
Pensiones:			
Islas Galápagos	1st.	Cuenca s/n	520203
Cabañas:			
Don Jorge	1st.	Vía Playa Man	520208

Source: CETUR (Corporación Ecuatoriana de Turismo) - 1998